I0123970

Unlimited Resources:

Simple and Easy Ways to Find, Access, and Utilize Client Strengths and Resources to Facilitate Change

Paul J. Leslie

Unlimited Resources: Simple and Easy Ways to Find, Access, and Utilize Client Strengths and Resources to Facilitate Change

Disclaimer:

The information in this book is not intended to be a substitute for consulting with your medical professional about your specific health condition. See your medical professional about any specific questions you have about your personal health.

Book Design by RamaJon - Bikeapelli Press, LLC

Cover Design by Meghan Benge www.meghanbenge.com

Path Notes Press books are available for order through Ingram Press Catalogues

Printed in the United States of America

ISBN: 978-0-9975950-2-4

OTHER BOOKS BY PAUL J. LESLIE

Potential Not Pathology: Helping Your Clients Transform Using Ericksonian Psychotherapy

The Year of Living Magically: Practical Ways to Create a Life of Spirit, Wonder, and Connection

Low Country Shamanism: An Exploration of Magical and Healing Practices of the Coastal Carolinas and Georgia

Get Out of Your Seat: An Average Passenger's Guide to Overcoming Airline Terror (with Ian Cox)

Acknowledgments

I want to thank all my friends and colleagues who have stood by me and championed my work over the years. There are far too many of you to list, but please know that you all have a very special place in my heart.

I bow in deep gratitude to my therapy clients from whom I learned that love and compassion are more important to healing than any therapeutic techniques.

A special thank you to my parents, Paul and Sue Leslie, who have always been my greatest resources.

TABLE OF CONTENTS

INTRODUCTION

Imagine the freedom to letting go of static therapeutic treatments and beginning creative and spontaneous interventions which will allow your clients to transcend their presenting issues. What would it be like to go beyond techniques and playfully embrace the unknown where anything can happen? Ponder moving your clients to places where they will discover surprising and empowering ways to transform their lives.

Client transformations are what most of us wanted when we started on our path to become therapists. Unfortunately, somewhere along that path we have been led away from trusting the healer within in us in favor of strict treatment guidelines and specific technical applications. We have become mesmerized by evidence based interventions marketed as the only effective methods of bringing about change. As therapists, we often feel the stress of managing sessions according to the whims of government agencies and insurance companies while the focus of therapy is firmly centered on diagnostic labels which direct the therapist to work within the frame of pathology rather than healing.

My goal is to introduce you to a different way of conducting therapy. This way will not limit the therapeutic practitioner to rigid adherence to any specific model of intervention. Instead, this approach allows the therapist the opportunity for greater observance of what is "right" with the client rather than what is in need of repair. By changing the focus of a therapy session, both client and therapist can begin to experience new and surprising opportunities to move toward healing. I call this a Resource Directed approach to Therapy.

Resource Directed Therapy (RDT) is a very practical way of working with clients that is based on the concept of directing the therapy process on the unique and powerful resources each person brings into the therapy session. Client resources are anything that contributes to the client's ability to move through life in a healthy, positive manner. The emphasis of this approach is on working within resourceful contexts while paying limited amounts of attention to the problems the client presents. Any event has the potential to be a resource depending on the context in which it is presented.

From a Resource Directed perspective, the purpose of therapy is to move an event from a problem context to a resource context. Once the context has changed, clients will have more access to the innate healing that resides within them. The therapist is called upon to take any action necessary, within ethical boundaries, to move clients outside of the limiting contexts they find themselves within. By limiting continual investigation of the client's problem and instead directing attention toward certain resourceful client actions, ideas or feelings, a shift occurs which causes the manner in which the client interacts with the problem. When this happens the client's ability to transform becomes easier.

I began exploring therapy from a resource directed perspective when I was conducting extensive research on the work of Dr. Milton Erickson. Erickson, who was a psychiatrist, had the most remarkable methods of creating change in his clients. His interventions sometimes seemed nonsensical, bizarre or ridiculous. In spite of the odd directives he gave, his success rate was remarkable. At first, Erickson's work was completely confusing to me. I wanted to understand how these strange directives could yield such amazing results in such short time spans. I was perplexed to say the least. The more I read about Erickson and investigated his approach, the more confused I became.

One day while reading about one of Erickson's cases I had an insight about how he conducted his work. Erickson was always moving people toward a new context of how they could live their lives. He was consistently directing them toward their resources and away from their problems. He did not directly attempt to solve his clients' problems. Instead, he gave them access to their own inner resources which allowed them to transcend their problems. He did anything he could to open up his clients to resources which could assist them in directing their own lives. Rather than focusing on the minutia of the problem, Erickson saw a bigger picture. He saw that his clients had unlimited resources at their command. Erickson's primary goal was to move his clients out of their impoverished view of their situation into a more resourceful way of interacting with life by most any means possible.

Once I really understood this aspect of Erickson's therapeutic orientation, I began shifting away from problem focus in my own work as a therapist (for the record after studying Erickson for many years, I am still both awed and baffled by his genius and his unique methods of working with people). Overnight, therapy became much different for me. I began to see change take place more quickly in sessions with my clients. My interventions became more directive but yet did not feel as if I was pushing my clients to change. I began to trust myself more as a therapist and often was even surprised by what came out of my own mouth when I was giving directives. Therapy became an interaction of healing rather than a technique driven, medical model of client "labeling" with strict guidelines on how to fix what was wrong.

I remember sitting in clinical supervision sessions hearing various cases in which most of what I heard was the constant focus and discussion on the pathology of the clients and little or no interest in client resources. These readily available resources which could bring about positive change were often ignored. Many of these wonderfully well-meaning therapists were stuck in a mindset that believes that insight and interpretation of the problem is the only way to move the client out of the problem. They also believed if what they were doing was not working, it was because either, the client was being resistant or the therapists did not have the right tool or technique to assist the client. However, I felt the real reason for failure to help create change in the client was that both the client and the therapist had become stuck in the very problem they were trying to solve. As a friend of mine told me once, "How can you help someone get out of a deep hole if you are down in that same hole with them?"

What I am offering is not a new "theory" or "technique". It is only a concept that can be applied from many different technical and theoretical orientations. This concept is not something that is offered in the psychotherapy marketplace as the latest and greatest new discovery. There are no expensive, elaborate trainings needed or certifications to be obtained. This is merely my way of introducing an old concept into a new era. Others before me have championed the need for resource directed applications to therapy, but were often overshadowed by more pathology focused practices. My thinking on the importance of shifting therapy away from a focus on problems was solidified in the works of Bateson (1972), Haley (1990), Madanes (2006), O'Hanlon (2003), and Ray and Keeney (1993). I found through their work a common thread of directing clients toward strengths and away from pathology emphasis. Instead of the familiar therapeutic investigation methods for dealing with problems, these practitioners and theorists sought unique ways to shift contexts and interactions within the therapy room which moved their clients toward positive, resourceful states.

I truly believe that if we as therapists can make a collective shift from the mindset of therapy as a left brained problem solving procedure to a right brained creative search for resources, then we will have better outcomes. We will also experience the kind of healing interactions we sought when we entered the field and this doesn't mean we throw out our techniques or theories but rather use them in a context which encourages movement toward client strengths rather than client deficiencies.

I wanted this book to be easily and quickly read as I understand most therapists are very busy and need good information in a short period of time. You will find limited citations and little extensive theoretical explorations. I want the reader to understand the basic concept without having to endure a marathon of reading and researching. I offer this simple work as an idea to enhance whatever methods the therapist is already successfully performing in his or her therapy sessions. This is just a map of how to navigate therapeutic interaction, and like any map, it is merely a guide on how to move from place to another.

Chapter one will provide the reasoning for adopting a Resource Directed approach to working with clients. I will present examples of how excessive investigation of the origin of the client's presenting issue can often limit the resolution of the problem and how changing the direction toward client resources can create remarkable shifts in client outcomes.

Chapter two presents the therapeutic presuppositions of performing Resource Directed Therapy. These presuppositions include a focus on client potential rather than client pathology, making the therapy session an alive, experiential process of interaction, focus on outcomes not origins, and orientation toward future possibilities instead of present issues.

Chapter four will examines what specifically are client resources and how to obtain them. In this chapter the concept of utilizing positive resources for quickly moving clients out of a problem context and into a new empowering context is elaborated upon.

Chapter six examines the crucial concept of context and its reframing in therapy. By utilizing what the client presents in therapy, the therapist can reframe meaning and actions into new contexts which can create shifts in beliefs and behaviors. Several methods of reframing and changing contexts are presented for the reader to use in his or her therapy sessions.

Chapter three, five, and seven present real case transcripts in which Resource Directed Therapy was utilized, Accompanying commentary is supplied to point out where and how resources are being accessed and utilized

In this book I have included many case studies since I have been told by other therapists that this is how they best learn. I also have included transcripts of some of my cases in which utilization of clients' resources made all the difference in how deeply and how quickly they healed. I am fortunate that in the last few years I have been able to apply the concept of Resource Directed Therapy to a wide variety of individuals and families whose problems range from slight to severe. I am grateful to my clients since they have helped me to learn more about myself through our interactions. Their openness to taking actions which initially appeared strange or silly and their willingness to reconsider their world in a different context has been inspiring to me. I am forever in their debt.

CHAPTER 1: THE PROBLEM WITH PROBLEM DIRECTED THERAPY

As therapists we are taught to look for what is wrong with our clients. From the first days of graduate school (or earlier) our attention is constantly directed toward zeroing in on what is considered dysfunctional in our clients. In graduate school we take classes which include such words as "Diagnostic", "Pathology" and "Assessment". In fact, it often appears that the field of psychotherapy is firmly focused on the problems our clients bring with them to therapy sessions.

We as therapists are expected to spot and then diagnose what is wrong with the client and propose a set plan of treatment so that the client will begin to function in a more effective manner. We spend much time in the search for etiology of what is causing our clients to seek "treatment." We hope that by finding the root cause of our clients' suffering we can formulate a solution which can assist clients change into normal, healthy people (whatever that is).

The problem with searching for causes and the labeling dysfunction as disorders is that often the more we focus on the problem the client brings, the more we become less effective therapists. We can become frozen inside a stagnant interaction that consists of an endless loop of problem thoughts, problem behaviors, and problem emotions. We often find it difficult to move the clients away from their problems if the majority of the time we therapists continue to explore the very thing the client wants to avoid. By constantly examining the problem and searching for the root cause of the problem, we leave little room for escape from the problem. If both the client and the therapist are mired in the context of the problem, then it is unlikely that any amount of goal setting or solution seeking will create a major shift in the client's life.

We may ask ourselves, "If I don't focus on the problem, then how will I know what the cause is so I can change it?" The simple answer is: you don't. When you shift your direction in therapy away from excessive problem investigation, you will find that you don't do most of the things you have learned in graduate school. You don't do many of the things you learned in continuing education courses. You don't plan a strict "treatment" as you have been instructed in the past. You don't follow rigid theoretical models of therapy as you have previously been educated. In essence, you don't do therapy as it is traditionally taught.

Before you sharpen your sword and skewer me on the altar of evidence-based peer reviewed models of treatment, hear me out. I have come not to bury psychotherapy, but to praise it. I praise the spirit of therapy which is rooted in healing and change. I love the impact good therapy can have on the quality of people's lives. I am inspired by how many wonderful, well-meaning therapists work so hard every day to assist their clients in transcending the challenges these clients face. It warms my heart to think about the care and compassion professionals in the field of psychotherapy demonstrate as they work tirelessly in helping others live more empowered lives.

Having said that, I also believe that there is a much needed change in the way we do therapy. If we want to preserve the spirit of healing which motivated so many of us to go into the field, we must move into the realm of right brain, creative heart centered and inspired approaches to therapy. Strict application of left brained, quantitative and standardized models can often limit the therapist's ability to generate change in a dynamic way.

One of the major impediments to successful outcomes in therapy is the clinician's consistent focus on the problem presented in the therapy session. When therapists continue to focus all their attention on what is wrong with the client, they begin to limit their ability to assist the client in creating new possibilities for him or herself. To make matters worse, the forced inclusion of strict, standardized methods of interacting with clients only continues to spotlight the problem. To move clients toward new possibilities and healing, it is important that our focus as therapists moves away from the standard problem directed approaches to client interaction and instead move toward a resource directed approach.

Resource Directed Therapy (RDT) shifts the attention of both the client and the therapist to anything that can contribute positively to the client's life. By shifting the attention from the troubling aspects of a client's life to a more positive resource, we indirectly give the client the ability to transform in surprising ways. This approach can appear almost counter intuitive to our trained pathology based approach to assisting clients. So much of our training has ingrained in us a reflexive move toward investigating our clients' problems and then searching for a solution for these problems.

This change of focus entails seeing within whatever problem the client brings to therapy as having the potential to be shifted into a resource. If therapy is focused around directing clients away from their problem and toward resources, the interaction between clients and therapist shifts from a limited, technique driven interaction into a lively, spontaneous interaction that can go in surprising directions.

A resource can be an emotion, experience, belief or

behavior that a client has experienced that can assist him or her in healing. Working from a resource directed perspective, the therapist is constantly seeking what the client already possesses or has experienced that can help move the client to positive outcomes in therapy. When a therapy session becomes centered on the client's resources, the client often finds the inner capability to change in, at times, astonishing ways.

Often a problem will continue to be maintained even when solutions are suggested. The circular interaction of problem solving in a therapy session can result in further attention and focus on the problem. To quote Keeney and Keeney (2012), "externalizing a problem or claiming that the problem is the problem contributes to problem saturated discourse. Worse, if the problem is ridiculed, scorned, or attacked, the systemic weave that holds its presence is fractionated and reduced to another dualism that is even more ready to perpetuate suffering in other life challenges" (p. 59).

It is not uncommon for therapists to experience burn out when day after day they search for solutions to the problems they are presented. By actively seeking solutions for clients, therapists often exert more energy than the clients themselves. The more the therapist stays in the frame of a problem the longer and more tedious the interaction with the client can be. Shifting the direction of a session from problem investigation to an investigation of resources can have startling effects as clients often seem to magically find their own solutions and even experience major shifts in problems which had appeared insurmountable to them.

Rather than searching for solutions, therapists can instead direct a client toward a resource which the client needs to heal him or herself. For example, I once worked with a client who had severe anxiety and had a problem sitting still and focusing. Her mind would race with erratic shifts in thinking and emotion and her body would follow along. Rather than search for a cause or a solution to her anxiety problem, I wanted her to experience the resource of being still, quiet, and reflective so she was given a set of crayons with two large coloring books. She was instructed that every morning before she left her house she was to take 10-15 minutes to color in the coloring books. She could pick any picture in the coloring book she wanted and choose any color she wanted to use. She was directed to ensure that each picture was thoroughly colored. Each part of a picture, which had a different color, must have a uniform look with the same even color which meant she must not bear too hard or too soft with the crayons when she was coloring. I told her that she could feel as anxious as she wanted during that time and could think any thoughts she wanted, but she was to do the coloring assignment every day for two weeks.

When she returned to therapy in two weeks she reported that she had done the assignment as directed and showed me her work. The pictures were neatly colored with as much uniform texture as possible. She had stayed within all the lines of the pictures and had used many different colors. She reported that she had begun to look forward to her morning coloring sessions because the act of focusing on the pictures allowed her to "turn off her brain" a little. She noticed she felt a little calmer and less jittery throughout her day. It was decided that she would continue her coloring for fifteen minutes in the morning and fifteen minutes in the evening. After another therapy session or two she found that she was better able to focus on her daily tasks and paid less attention to her racing thoughts. Her assignment, in which she could channel her attention on one single task, allowed her to use her own resources in controlling her anxiety. She indirectly discovered that she had some degree of control over her thinking and her actions.

In order to help clients gain access to resources which will enable them to transcend the problems which brought them to therapy, sessions need to be geared toward moving the client out of the context of a problem. The therapist must take an active part in directing the sessions toward any resources which can assist clients in breaking out of their limited problem focused perspective.

The following are examples of the differences between a problem directed session and a resource directed session:

A client seeks help due to his excessive stress and anger regarding his work. He works many hours for a boss who shows little concern for the client's well-being. The boss constantly adds more work on top of the already excessive amount of work the client is already doing. The client is having trouble sleeping and is often exhausted. He is very angry and has been taking out his frustration on his family by having outbursts of anger which result in fights between himself and his wife.

A problem directed session could look something like this:

Client: I am so angry at my boss! He is totally oblivious to what I am going through. I can't perform with this kind of effort for much longer. Nobody seems to care about the employees! We all want to do a good job, but we can only do so much.

Therapist: It sounds like you are really upset and you feel mistreated.

Client: I do!

Therapist: How angry do you get when you think about how this situation is playing out?

Client: I get very angry! It is just not fair.

Therapist: Your relationship with your boss is very contentious.

Client: Yes.

Therapist: What other people have you experienced this kind of contention with in the past?

The well-meaning therapist has decided to direct the session toward further exploration of the client's anger guaranteeing to keep both parties firmly locked in the context of therapy as an exploration of an anger problem.

Another problem directed session might look like this:

Client: I am so angry at my boss! He is totally oblivious to what I am going through. I can't perform with this kind of effort for much longer. Nobody seems to care about the employees! We all want to do a good job, but we can only do so much.

Therapist: That sounds awful. Have you tried talking with your boss about how you feel?

Client: Yes, but I get his condescending attitude when I tell him that I am already overworked. He just doesn't seem to care. I don't know if there is anything I can do at this point.

Therapist: Have you tried giving him some clear examples of how you could be more efficient in your job if you had a little breathing room?

Client: I have tried to talk to him so many times, but his answer is always the same.

Therapist: Have you thought about approaching him with another employee who also feels the same?

Client: I could, but I don't want to make him angry and think that I am trying to avoid work.

This therapist is working very hard to find a solution to the client's problem; however, this does not yield results and even locks the interaction further into the realm of a problem.

In contrast let us examine a possible interaction with a Resource Directed Therapist:

Client: I am so angry at my boss! He is totally oblivious to what I am going through. I can't perform with this kind of effort for much longer. Nobody seems to care about the employees! We all want to do a good job, but we can only do so much.

Therapist: You say that with a lot of authority in your voice.

Client: Yeah, because I am really upset with the whole situation.

Therapist: I bet you are the kind of person who doesn't just stand by and let people be mistreated. I bet you are someone who stands up to injustice.

Client: Well, I guess I do

Therapist: Yeah. You sound like the kind of person who could bring about a large change in the world. Are you involved in any humanitarian projects?

Client: No. I don't have time to do much with my work schedule.

Therapist: I understand, but with your passion for standing up for people I think you would have a lot to offer others.

Client: I have wanted to get involved in working with my kids' school system. There are a lot of things that I think could be changed to make things better. I want my kids to have as good an education as possible.

Therapist: Your children are really important to you, aren't they?

Client: Yes they are. They are the reason I work as hard as I do.

Therapist: A lot of parents could learn from your example and maybe even benefit from your guidance. Your work ethic is so strong, and your desire to help others is so obvious. I can see why your boss doesn't worry about whether you can handle all that work.

Client: It is a lot of work, but I do the best I can with it.

Now the session has departed from the realm of the problem and shifted into the realm of a resource. The client's resources of being a good parent, hard worker and a humanitarian gives the therapist an exit from the heavy and limited perspective of overwork and powerlessness. Further explorations of the client's past history and formulating solutions for his problem could possibly cement the problem in his consciousness.

Another possible resource directed interaction:

Client: I am so angry at my boss! He is totally oblivious to what I am going through. I can't perform with this kind of effort for much longer. Nobody seems to care about the employees! We all want to do a good job, but we can only do so much.

Therapist: That is really intense the way you said that. Have you ever thought of taking acting lessons?

Client: No.

Therapist: You might consider doing that. All that energy could be used in a powerful way. You could really move an audience with that kind of intensity.

Client: I don't think I want to be an actor.

Therapist: Maybe a political leader? I just hear a lot of energy in the way you speak.

Client: I wish I were in charge of the political process.

Therapist: Well, with that kind of energy, I bet a lot of people would follow you.

By shifting the direction of therapy away from excessive problem investigation or excessive solution exploration, the space for transformation opens up. By moving the therapy session toward client strengths and resources, new possibilities can emerge which might not happen if the focus of the session was only directed toward client weaknesses and deficiencies. Just the act of discussing a potential client resource can often have a dramatic effect in how a client begins to perceive his or her problem.

Please do not think that I am advocating for totally ignoring the problem or not letting clients tell their story. I am not promoting an absolutistic view of therapy. There may be times in which solutions could be sought and clients' past history can be explored; however, these actions might be more effective if the sole focus of the therapy session is not on clients' limitations and complications. By accessing clients' resources in the session it allows them to more fully find their own solutions and even deal with past issues more effectively.

Many therapists believe that client resources are compartmentalized into only one small area of a client's life. If the client does not have a resource they need within the problem situation, then it is assumed that further exploration and application of therapeutic techniques within the frame of the problem will be the only way to assist the client in exiting this limited frame. In contrast, the resources which clients experience in other areas of their life can overlap into the problem frame. When this occurs it is often easier to create change by focusing on a more resourceful part of the client's life. When certain behaviors, attitudes, or emotions are activated in one area of a person's life, those same resources can be utilized in other areas.

A good example of pulling resources from one area to be utilized in another area is a case of a young man who sought out Milton Erickson for help. The young man was unable to cross crowded, busy streets. In their discussion, Erickson learned that the young man's avoidance of crowded areas was due to his fear of any kind of interaction with women. Erickson focused their therapeutic sessions on assisting the young man improve his physique. Due to Erickson's encouragement, the young man began to develop his strength and muscle thus improving his overall body image. As a result of his improved body image, the young man developed much more confidence about his body which led to his changing other areas of his life, including leaving his mother's home, getting his own apartment, and walking down crowded streets (Haley, 1973).

In a similar example, I once worked with a man who was going through a divorce. His wife had decided she did not want to be married to him and had left him to move back home with her parents. Even though he knew her decision was for the best, it still left him with very little confidence in himself and an aching heart. He was depressed and alone which resulted in his becoming more isolated and feeling more hopeless about his life. In talking with him, I found that he had wanted to be a stand-up comedian and writer. He had mostly given up on his dream and felt trapped working a job he didn't like and having very little time for anything other than work.

After listening to his problem and validating his feelings, the next step was to help him design a way to get back to his dream of becoming a comedian. Even though he couldn't seem to understand why we were focusing on his dream instead of his ending marriage, my client took to the assignment very quickly. Ideas about how to land comedy gigs were brainstormed and were put into systematic action steps for him to complete over the next two weeks between sessions. We came up with ideas about how he could use social media to post videos and samples of his writing to attract attention to his comedy skills. He came up with a variety of new skits based on these brainstorming sessions which he happily put into practice in his new routines. He became energetic and enthusiastic while we worked to steer him back to his dream.

After four sessions, he felt he was in a good place and did not need to return to therapy. He felt that, even though he missed his wife, he could go on to live an amazing life by himself. By focusing our sessions on his resources of creativity and humor, he was able to find confidence in himself. He would follow his dream with the confidence that he had something to offer the world even if his wife was not in his life. He also began to trust himself more and to even interact with others more often. By leaving the realm of the problem labeled "divorce" and instead moving toward his resource of confidence, he began reclaiming his life and moving into the future.

When attention is directed toward client resources, sessions are opened up to allow a flow of interaction which can invoke great shifts in how clients experience their lives. Some of the most inspiring stories of healing in our field rarely come from excessive problem investigation. Remarkable things can happen when a therapist treats therapy as an experiential interaction which can result in clients gaining resources to which they previously had limited access. Once clients are directed toward those resources they can begin to heal without the need for a standard treatment model based on a strict method of administration.

One of the most inspiring cases in which a client's whole life was transformed by shifting attention toward a resource was the classic case of Milton Erickson and the African Violet Queen. Erickson was approached by a friend who knew Erickson was giving a presentation in Milwaukee. His friend asked Erickson to visit his aunt about whom the friend was very worried. The aunt, who had been a vivacious woman most of her life, had recently started having some severe health issues which resulted with her confined to a wheelchair. This turn of events had caused her to become very depressed. She lived alone in a huge house she had inherited and did not have any interaction with the outside world anymore due to her being immobile. She had become depressed and her nephew, fearing the worse, approached Erickson for help. Erickson agreed to see the aunt between his scheduled lectures.

When Erickson arrived at the woman's home, he noticed how dismal and dark the home looked and how it appeared to be frozen in time with nothing changed other than adjustments made for the accessibility of her wheelchair. As the woman took Erickson around her home, he noticed that the only place he saw any evidence of happiness was the greenhouse which the woman proudly showed to Erickson. He saw that she put much effort in to working with the plants in her nursery, and he was particularly impressed with the vast number of African Violets that she had grown. It was apparent to Erickson that working in the nursery and planting those African Violets was the only place in the woman's life where she had any sense of happiness.

In talking with the woman, Erickson learned that she used to be very active in many social activities, specifically in her church. She told Erickson that since she had become disabled she had ceased all church activity and was indeed, very depressed. Erickson told the woman that depression was not her problem; her problem was that she had not been a very good Christian. The woman was very surprised to hear this comment and took offense. Erickson continued by telling her that with all the beautiful plants she had raised, it was not very Christian of her to refuse to share those gorgeous gifts with others who need beauty in their lives. He directed her to look through the church bulletin which was mailed to her, and look for any announcements of births, deaths, or anniversaries. She was then to take one of the many African Violets to the family mentioned in the announcement.

The woman thought about what Erickson had said and agreed to take a clipping of one of her violets to everyone mentioned in the bulletin. Many years later, when the woman passed away the headline in the local newspaper read "African Violet Queen of Milwaukee Dies, Mourned by Thousands." By directing this woman to resources she already possessed, Erickson was not only able to help her alleviate her depression, but to also give her a profound sense of meaning and purpose in life. When asked by students why he focused on her African Violets, Erickson replied that he looked at her life and thought it might be easier to grow the African violets part of her life rather than to weed out the depression (Gordon & Meyers Anderson, 1981).

By adopting a mindset that shifts the direction of therapy away from client limitations and toward client resources, the therapist is presented with more freedom to explore other areas of their clients' lives which could yield great value to therapeutic outcomes. If therapy is solely concentrated on clients' dysfunction and the fixing of such dysfunction, other empowering resources which could be of immense value to clients could be obscured. Opening ones' mind to the possibility of viewing the therapy process in a Resource Directed way does not mean to stop performing techniques which have been shown to help clients. It simply means that those techniques and applications could be utilized in a more positive, life enhancing interaction.

CHAPTER 2: PRESUPPOSITIONS FOR PERFORMING RESOURCE DIRECTED THERAPY

In order to cultivate a resource directed approach to performing therapy, it would be wise to adopt some presuppositions about the therapy process. By adopting these presuppositions, one can gain greater flexibility and effectiveness in dealing with whatever may occur in a therapy session. The act of shifting our perspective away from a limiting problem based model of intervention can open the door to unforeseen ways that people can change. Our assumptions about therapy can be the most important aspect in our interactions with clients. If our assumptions about the therapeutic process are bound by a habitual searching for problems, we will usually get what we seek. If on the other hand, we look at therapy as a powerful, life changing interaction, we may surprise ourselves at how creative and resourceful we, as therapists, can become.

Assisting your clients in accessing their own resources in order to create change should not be something radically different to us. Unfortunately, many therapists lose this perspective due to their work environments which insist on analyzing, critiquing and attempting to eradicate client problems. It is very easy to lose sight of the bigger picture of healing. When therapists allow their therapy sessions to become lively, energetic interactions which search for resources instead of problems, the outcome is often an increase in creativity and spontaneity on the part of both therapists and clients.

The following presuppositions are recommended to begin changing the perspective to performing therapy. These are not facts or techniques, but merely ideas which can benefit any practitioner of the therapeutic arts to become more creative and resourceful in interactions with clients.

Presupposition #1: Therapy is best when it focuses on client potential not client pathology

Our focus in a therapy session determines where our clients place their focus long after they leave the therapy session. As Corbett (2011) puts it, "psychotherapists subtly train the people with whom they work to talk about some things more than others, depending on the material to which the therapist pays particular attention" (p.45). By being aware of where we place our attention, we can begin to create a space of transformation for the people we help. If we focus our attention on client deficits, we are sure to find many of them. Hunting for pathology guarantees its appearance.

"Any effort to discover pathology will contribute to the creation of that pathology" – Bradford Keeney

While I was writing a book on the work of Milton Erickson the phrase "potential not pathology" popped into my mind, and it became the title of the book. I also believe that potential is a crucial guiding principle of a resource directed approach to therapy. When we focus our attention on what is wrong with our clients, we are very susceptible to becoming locked into an unbalanced view of the person with whom we are working. The client is neither a disorder nor a set of assumptions about etiology.

The more we look at our clients as a walking diagnostic label, the more we are drawn to explore this label and, in turn, what is "wrong" with them. If we go beyond the labels of "bipolar", "borderline", "generalized anxiety", etc., we find there are real human beings in the therapy room who have access to resources that they can activate to begin living their lives in more dynamic ways. By needlessly identifying clients with their symptoms, we make it more difficult for us, as therapists, to discover those resources. Even worse is when clients begin to identify with the very labels that well-meaning mental health professionals placed on them. To quote Lankton (2001), "traditional therapy is based on the assumption of an objective reality that is independent of our efforts to observe it. The posture toward reality is separation from it and study by reduction. But while the simple act of reduction and labeling seems innocent enough, it does not credit the observer with the action of inventing the label that is applied. Furthermore, this description often pathologizes the individual and typically excludes his or her current life context" (p.195).

My experience is that the people who have the most trouble making positive changes in their lives are often the ones who have identified with their "problem" so much that they feel that if they change, they will cease to be who they are. When clients take on the identity of their problems, it is difficult for them to consider the possibility that their lives could be different. Consciously, clients may desire to be different, but unconsciously they are limited in their options because of their sense of identity is invested in the problem. If clients have invested their identity into being the "the "depressed person", the" bipolar person", or the "anorexic person", it is more difficult to shift the focus away from that fixed state of identity.

As Boscoloe and Bertrando (1996) point out, a focus on a diagnostic label "leads to reification and the consequent simplification of a complex reality. Sometimes this reification has drastic pragmatic effects. This is because a diagnosis, particularly a severe diagnosis, can introduce an idea of timelessness. Once a diagnosis has been stated, it tends to become part of the identity of the person, and the person will never get rid of it….the diagnosis may also translate into an all-encompassing idea, in which the person becomes the illness and the illness becomes the person" (p.49).

In order to help people, we must train ourselves to decrease our focus on dysfunction. We must remind ourselves that our clients do have access to incredible resources for healing. In assisting our clients to discover and access their own resources for growth and change, we must consistently focus our attention on the strengths that the client already possesses. We must direct clients back to these resources even as life's tragedies prevents their remembering how to connect to them. Excessive labeling of pathology can often freeze a client in the realm of pathology which can block access mental and emotional resources which could be used for healing. As Corbett (2011) states, "it is increasingly recognized that an exclusive focus on psychopathology gives us a distorted view of the personality" (p.8). By redirecting our clients (and ourselves) to investigate their innate strengths, we can remind them that they have a vast repository of resources which can be utilized to make changes in their emotions and actions. Cozolino (2004) reminds therapists, "in your quest to diagnose and treat pathology, remember that every client possesses at least one strength. Whether that strength is a musical talent, the love of a pet, or a burning passion to ride motorcycles, it may boost self-esteem or motivate change" (p.53).

Sarah came to therapy after she was released from the hospital. She had been there for a week due to expressing suicidal ideation because of her severe depression. She presented her file to me which was a long list of all the various diagnoses and treatments which had been used while she was hospitalized. She clearly told me that she had been diagnosed with Bipolar II, Generalized Anxiety Disorder, and Obsessive Compulsive Disorder. She was overwhelmed by her life and had been going to therapy for several years in the hopes she could change. She told me about the hopelessness she felt being Bipolar and how she couldn't seem to get past how it felt to be labeled as "a serious mental health case."

After listening to her story for a few minutes, I asked her, when she wasn't being a serious mental health case, what activities did she enjoy. She said she enjoyed drawing, painting and interacting with her children. I asked her when was the last time she was really focused on something that was very creative. She thought for a few moments and then told me it had been a long time. With all the troubles she had the last few years with her mental health issues, she had not really focused on doing as many creative things as she once had. She even appeared to mourn the loss of her old life, which included more time to draw and have fun with artistic endeavors.

I wondered out loud to her whether she was really a serious mental health case, or just experiencing a serious lack of creativity case. I asked if she had ever thought that her creativity disappearing might have had some connection with her mental health issues. She replied that she had never thought about any connection between the two. I began to describe great artists throughout history who had appeared unstable to the general public but yet their perceived instability may have been how they accessed their creativity in dramatic ways. I suggested that creative people often appear so different to others that they often have all sorts of labels applied to them, none of which are flattering.

This line of thinking seemed to hit Sarah pretty hard. She suddenly spoke up with a smile, "Do you mean that maybe if I can stay creative I will feel better?" "Maybe", I said, "but you have to realize that every intensely creative person will have ebbs and flows of creativity. Life is a flowing experience not a set, static way. There will be times when you feel incredibly creative, and you may want to create more things than you can imagine. However, as with all things, there will be times when the creativity will appear to stop, but only temporarily. It is kind of the like the ocean, in that when the tide comes in it comes in with such power. It is an awe inspiring sight. However, the tide also goes out in a soft quiet way. It is almost as if the tide needs to pull away and be quiet in order to recharge itself. This may be the way you are. You come in with such a creative force that you create a sense of awe, but then after a while, you can feel yourself draw back into a quiet place where you need to recharge. Sometimes that recharging process can feel dark and painful, yet it may be necessary in order for the waves to come back with such amazing creativity."

Sarah sat quietly as she reflected on what I had said. She had been told by many well-meaning mental health professionals that she was "a serious mental health case." However, now she was seeing herself as more than a "label" of various diagnostic classifications. She asked me how she could learn to work with these tides of creativity. We began to design a plan that would accommodate these creative changes in her life. We first decided that she was to immediately begin creating artwork again, even if she was not inspired. I told her that she was free to throw away anything she didn't like, but she had to let her creative side know that it was being supported by her so that it wouldn't continue to hide. We also designed a procedure in which when she knew the tides of creativity were going out, she had access to support and to understanding individuals who realized that this was part of her "natural, creative cycle."

In time, Sarah learned to have better control over her fluctuating emotional states by paying more attention to her creative side. When she began to experience the early signs of depression, which was relabeled a charging period, she connected with family and friends who assisted her through those darker days. Even though she still had issues with her moods, instead of being a mental health label or a "serious case," she was able to find meaning and purpose in her creative work. By accepting the suggestion that she was a creative person who had creative moods, she began to improve and eventually even thrive in many areas of her life.

More and more mental health practitioners are growing concerned about the rampant diagnosing that is required in the mental health field. Many diagnoses make normal human reactions to situational distress something labeled a disorder and pathological. The need to diagnose clients with a disorder label for payment by insurance companies has been around for many years. I have known many therapists who moved away from taking insurance so as not to label their clients with a diagnosis of being "sick".

Some questions to ponder: What would it be like not to have to answer to insurance companies and move past diagnostic labels? What if all one had to do was just treat clients instead of categorizing them as a diagnostic code? Would moving past rampant diagnosing allow us to see the potential rather than the pathology in our clients? Could we see a client's life as an unfolding masterpiece rather than a label of illness?

Presupposition #2: For maximum effectiveness, don't do therapy, BE therapy

We all have seen therapy sessions in which therapists and clients have sedate conversations which appear to go nowhere, but if there is no life or energy in a therapy session, then one can be assured that the session contains little or no healing. If therapists do not generate the conditions for healing to occur by their mere presence, then it is up to the clients to do it. However, clients are unable to generate a state of healing, otherwise they would not be seeking therapy in the first place. It is in the experience of interaction that great changes can occur.

Our being detached as outside observers of the healing process does not often create substantial changes in our clients. If your goal as a therapist is to follow rigid patterns and not to create a space for "magic" to occur, then you may want to reconsider your profession. Often it is the interaction with the therapist which causes a shift in a client. From a resource directed perspective, therapy is a synergetic process which requires therapists to become an active part of the process, not an observer interpreting what they observe. In this lively interaction, the therapist has become an integral part of the change process. The therapists' actions create new, spontaneous interventions which move clients toward surprising outcomes. The free flow of information between therapists and clients enable exciting shifts in how the client experiences the problem for which they seek help.

As of late, many studies on psychotherapy, particularly those on evidence-based practices, appear to edit out the role of the therapist in therapeutic interactions. It was found that many studies measuring the effectiveness of psychotherapy often overlooked the importance of the therapist in preference to the measurement of theoretical models (Sprenkle & Blow, 2007; Blow, Sprenkle, and Davis, 2007). As Lebrow (2006) states, "psychotherapy researchers typically focus on different clinical interventions while ignoring the psychotherapists who make use of them. It's as if treatment methods were like pills, in no way affected by the person administering them. Too often researchers regard the skills, personality and experience of the therapist as side issues, features to control to ensure that different groups receive comparable interventions" (p.131).

The push for finding the "Holy Grail" of effective therapy often omits the most important element: the interaction. Somehow therapists have come to believe if they just have the right technique or theory, then they can be extremely effective. Anyone who has been in the field for a while knows that the difference between a good therapist and an ineffective therapist has little to do with strict theoretical orientations. According to Beutler, Malik, Alimohamed, Harwood, Talebi, Noble, and Wong (2004), "In efficacy research, the focus is on maximizing the power of treatments. Thus, efforts are made to control the influences of therapist factors by constructing treatment manuals that can be applied in the same way to all patients within a particular diagnostic group, regardless of any particular clinician. This research gives scant attention to any curative role that might be attributed to therapist factors that are independent of the treatment model and procedures" (p.227).

Our ability to facilitate change in our clients has more to do with our interaction "with" them rather than what we are doing "to" them, but the quest for measurable outcomes from insurance companies and health maintenance organizations has created a stampede in the psychotherapy marketplace. The seeking of the latest and greatest evidence based technical models often obscures the crucial element of therapist and client interaction. According to Fife, Whiting, Bradford, and Davis (2014), "effective therapy involves not only what we do, but who we are and how we regard our clients. The effective use of skills and techniques rests upon the quality of the therapist-client alliance, which in turn is grounded in the therapist's way of being, a concept that reflects a therapist's in-the-moment stance or attitude toward clients." (p.21)

For an understanding of how to use interaction based therapy which focuses on resources, it may be helpful to explore the concept of cybernetics and how this applies to therapeutic interventions. Cybernetics is an approach used to study the patterns of interdependence. In the 1960s and 1970s, cybernetics was explored by many therapists, particularly those from the systemic therapy and family therapy field. Unfortunately, cybernetics seems to have lost much of its impact upon the field of psychotherapy due to confusion about how it works and changes in the therapeutic marketplace.

Performing therapy from a cybernetic viewpoint is to observe the process of therapy from a holistic perspective. This view does not accept the standard model of seeing clients' symptoms as originating from a linear cause and effect model. It is more concerned with seeing clients in relationship with their environment, rather than considering them as existing in isolation. From this perspective, clients cannot exist without the presence of the environment. By only focusing on finding cause and effect processes, therapists direct their attention toward the perceived cause of the problem, while ignoring the context (societal, family, etc.) in which the problem has developed. A cybernetic perspective is more interested in observing the events which work together to create the problem as coordinated by a process of recursive feedback.

The role of cybernetics in therapy places more emphasis on the patterns of the problem, which are studied within the context in which the problem occurs, rather than the problem itself. With this emphasis, the focus of therapists is on the relationships and connections involved with the problem instead of on clients' symptoms. The whole of the event is considered greater than the parts because each part is only able to be understood and addressed in relation to the context of the whole. This is helpful because, if an individual part is a part of a greater whole, then a change in one part becomes a change in the whole as the whole regulates itself through feedback from its parts. The goal of the whole or "system" is to maintain its stability by taking in information from its parts. If information is fed into the system different from what has previously been used to regulate itself, then the system will have to adjust to accommodate this new information in order to maintain its stability.

This organization of information is a circular process because no one part creates another, but each individual part is connected in an interdependent manner to other parts. This circular process is in contrast to the linear cause and effect model in which X causes Y. In this model, "what we distinguish as cause and what we distinguish as effect is a matter of how we choose to punctuate the interaction" (Musikantow, 2011, p.84). A circular process, however, perceives that individuals in a therapy session are a part of a system that is maintained by circular feedback, with each individual responding to the other. The information generated in the interaction is then processed as feedback into the system. By simply redirecting clients away from excessive problem investigation by moving them toward resources, we then are altering the manner in which the system operates (Ray and Keeney, 1993).

Most of our thinking about the way we interact with our world is based on the premise that we are separate from the environment in which we exist. Bateson (1979) stated that things within a system are jointly defined, with each existing only in reference to the system's perceptions that provided them with definitions. There is not one specific part of a living, interacting system that can have complete dominance over any of the other parts of the system.

Bateson (1972) believed both therapist and client were one component and their interactions can create change and growth. Instead of classifying the client and the therapist as separate entities, the therapist will look for patterns which connect both parties. This creates a goal for the therapist to develop different patterns of interaction which will reduce the need for problematic behavior. In the therapeutic session, both clients and therapists are intertwined in a feedback process which makes both parties responsible for the direction of the session.

There are two levels of cybernetics: first order and second order. In first order cybernetics, therapists do not see themselves as part of the system that is being explored. Therapists operating in first order cybernetics will draw a distinction between themselves and the clients with whom they are interacting. At this level, therapists believe they are outside the phenomena being observed. In second order cybernetics, therapists recognize they are part of the phenomena being observed and understand the recursive nature of their interactions with their clients. From this perspective, therapists cannot view themselves as outside the system they are observing as they are a part of the patterns which are being observed (Keeney, 1983).

Since therapists are part of a feedback process, they must determine at what level a therapeutic intervention will be the most useful. Therapists must be willing to alter their own behavior in order to effectively create new patterns of interaction in the session, because the goal of the interaction is to change the configuration of the system that has been deemed problematic. If therapists' behaviors continue to maintain the feedback that stabilizes and maintains the problem, then therapists have now become part of the problem. Failing to consider that therapists are part of a feedback loop, means interventions can have limited impact upon the system. By making a shift in their own behavior, therapists can provide a change in the information presented to the system.

According to Keeney and Keeney (2012), the shifting of their own behaviors is the most therapists can do since the effects of their behavior can be used to create change, if indeed there is feedback between them and their clients. To operate within the system effectively, therapists need to be able to adjust their own behaviors and notice the effects these adjusts make with clients. Therapists who are sensitive to the feedback they receive from their clients during interactions and are able to adjust their own responses to that feedback, have been noted as a key quality to effectiveness in outcomes (Duncan, Miller, and Sparks, 2004).

Responding to and using what is offered by clients in a spontaneous manner in order to achieve positive therapeutic outcomes is known as "utilization". The concept of utilization comes from the work Milton Erickson. Utilization can be defined as "the acceptance and validation of any behavior, thought or emotion that a client exhibits as a foundation for creating a desired therapeutic outcome" (Leslie, 2014). Even if our client's offerings are dysfunctional or frustrating, by utilizing what is offered, the therapist is able to build an interaction which allows the therapist to channel the client's responses in more resourceful ways.

A resource directed therapist does not need to "do" therapy but rather "become" therapy. The therapist no longer sits outside the interaction as an observer offering up theoretical observations based on strict models of psychopathology. Instead, the therapist is co-creating a different way of interacting with the world along with the client. The therapist is actively participating in an experiential performance which results in clients experiencing the very resources they need to transform their lives while they are in the therapy session. In order to construct a life changing experience for the client, we, as therapists, need to change ourselves to evoke the needed resources within the client. Being a passive participant in therapy rarely leads to dramatic transformations. As Nardone (1996) states, "The therapist is both the director and the principal actor of the movie. He or she must possess refined technical preparation, great methodological rigor, a lively creativity, and a great mental flexibility. In other words the therapist must simultaneously be a scientist and an artist" (p. 69).

Keeney (2009) convincingly argues that therapy is more of a performance art rather than a strict social science, and it is the interaction between the performers (clients and therapist) which generates change rather than the rigid adherence to techniques or procedures. He writes: "Performed rather than interpreted, therapy cannot be reduced to any explanatory metaphor or pragmatic schema that will help a therapist know what to express. No matter

40

how hard you may try, you cannot jump out of the scene and avoid performing. Listening is an action and every effort not to influence, communicate, structure, or intervene becomes a paradoxical way of poorly doing the very thing you resist enacting" (p.35).

Commenting on his ground breaking interactive experiential work with families, Carl Whitaker stated, "As I take a position, an interactive process is triggered. My action begets their reaction. As they react, I respond to them and an interactive set is underway. Hopefully this dialectic will eventually lead to a higher order synthesis" (Whitaker & Bumberry, 1988, p.6). When we have decided to become therapy instead of doing therapy, we can no longer cling to set, structured pre-arranged methods which will inhibit our ability to be spontaneous. Understanding that each participant in the therapy process is unique, our interventions become much more than regurgitations of past therapists and theorists. When we understand that how we respond in a therapy session directly shifts the structure of the problem brought to be healed, we may find a greater sense of freedom in how we perceive the interactions in our therapy rooms. As Whitaker relates, "I'm not just acting in reaction to them, but I'm offering them a glimpse of my own internal responses as well. In other words, they're having the experience of my experience of me, not just feedback about them" (Whitaker & Bumberry, 1988, p.89).

I once worked with a woman who sought therapy for her anger issues. She really wanted to be able to control her anger, but she seemed unaware of how she sounded when she talked to people. She was very sharp in her tone and quick to snap at anyone when she was uncomfortable. By the time she realized she was snapping at her family or co-workers, it was often too late since she had hurt someone else's feelings. Once she saw what had happened, she then turned the anger on herself which led to emotional melt downs and self-loathing which fueled more anger inside. To her, this vicious cycle seemed to happen all by itself, and she felt powerless to change it. In therapy previously, she had learned about controlling her thinking patterns which had limited results for her as the vicious cycle seemed to happen before she could even think about it.

After the first few minutes of getting to know her and finding out what brought her to therapy, the woman became very flustered with trying to answer one of my questions which resulted in her getting upset and snapping at me. I immediately jumped out of my seat and ran and hid behind my chair. "What are you doing?" asked my client who was baffled by my odd behavior. "You are scary when you are angry, and I needed to hide." I said from behind the chair in a mock quivering voice. "This is ridiculous!" she snapped at me. "Maybe, but you are scary when you are angry," I replied. "Come on! You are being silly." my client said becoming frustrated by the fact that her therapist was not only acting oddly, but also not instantly responding to her orders. "I can't! I am too timid. You are scary and I am scared of you!" I said in a playful, childlike voice. For a moment the client grew quiet. "I guess this is how I make people feel when I get mad, huh?" she asked in a more relaxed tone. "Maybe," I said. As I peeked out from behind the chair I told her, "I will come out if you promise not to scare me." She agreed that she would do her best to not become angry with me. I came out from behind the chair and continued our discussion.

As this session and proceeding sessions continued, every time she started to become angry due to being flustered or uncomfortable, I would get up and hide behind the chair. This action then became a source of laughter for both of us. She became better at recognizing her emotional state. The biggest change came the day when she started to become frustrated and instead of snapping at me with anger, she grabbed a pillow from the couch she was sitting on and hid behind it. She laughed for a moment, and then something shifted inside her. She began to cry releasing years of hurt and pain which had been concealed inside the vicious cycle of anger and self-loathing. It was the playful interaction between us which gave her the tools to adjust her responses, not scripted theoretical information.

Presupposition #3: Therapy needs to be an experience

As much as I respect the many variations of talk therapy, I have often found that it can sometimes be very challenging to shift a person's perspective using only left-brained logic. I agree that by teaching clients (and maybe even arguing with them) about how they think, we can give them rational information about how to change their perspectives. Yet often, even though clients may know that they have a choice of what to believe and the role of their thinking on their quality of life, they still feel stuck in limiting beliefs about themselves and the world around them.

To remedy this type of situation, I have often found that an easier way to change clients' belief is to direct them to have an experience in which they are compelled to view their situation and themselves differently. Rather than struggling with getting clients to constantly question their thinking about a particular situation, I find that giving clients an "out of the ordinary" experience can have real generative effects on their beliefs.

Current research in the field of neuroscience suggests that novel experiences can alter gene expression which can have an

43

effect upon health and emotional well-being. It has also been found that negative experiences, such as intense social interactions and stress, can disrupt the process of development and growth of neurons called neurogenesis. Ernest Rossi, a leading researcher in the field of mind/body therapy, states, "the essence of psychotherapy becomes a process of facilitating "creative moments" that are encoded in new proteins and neural networks in the brain" (2001, p.155). He further expounds, "Experiencing creative moments is the phenomenological correlate of a critical change in the molecular structure of proteins within the brain associated with the creation of new cell assemblies, memory and learning. Molecular transformation in the brain in response to psychological shock, arousal and novelty is now recognized by the author as the deep psychobiological basis of psychopathology as well as the educational, constructive and synthetic approach to healing and psychotherapy" (2001, p.156).

Rossi spells it out for us that psychotherapy must be a process that actively generates creative novelty in order to have an impact on the brains of our clients. If this is the case, then it is no wonder that many therapists do not see the results in their work as they would like to see. Many therapists spend their time excavating their clients' history to find the origins of all the bad things brought into therapy. This problem focused perspective does little to create a new experience for the client. Too much time spent on problems solidifies problems, whereas a new experience can create a radical shift in perspective.

Few graduate programs teach beginning counselors to be novel and creative in order to assist clients in changing. If a major event or situation caused "psychological shock, arousal and/or novelty" in our clients and created negative issues then wouldn't clients need to experience a different kind of shock, arousal or novelty (the good kind) in therapy to activate their own resources in order to begin to heal? If clients get knocked off course by something different from what they usually experience, don't they need something different to put them back where they were? Carl Whitaker put it even more directly when he stated, "true emotional growth occurs only as a result of experience" (Whitaker and Bumberry, 1988, p.85).

Many of the legendary therapists we study before we enter the field gave their clients a unique experience to facilitate the psychobiological healing process. This type of creative novelty in therapy is not something that one can learn from a textbook. It must come from within the therapist. The only way to find out what kind of novel and creative things we can use in therapy is to roll up our sleeves and jump in. If the therapist truly "becomes" the therapy rather than merely regurgitating someone else's therapeutic guidelines, then it is much easier to access client resources.

Some ways to create shifts in a session:

-ask clients to change seats with the therapist if they always sit in the same place

-ask clients if the therapist can speak with an unusual accent for the whole session

-tell stories which emotionally move clients and gives them ideas on how to grow

-the therapist really laughs out loud when something funny happens in a session

-ask adult clients to color with crayons during the session so both therapist and client can relax

-write songs or poems with clients about their particular issue

-direct clients to conduct healing rituals to assist them in moving forward with their lives

-ask clients to write out their present issue as a television sitcom where each character gets a laugh

-tell the client that the therapist will be the depressed/anxious/etc. client in the session and the client can be the therapist

Therapists must feel free to come up with their own novel way of approaching therapy and then watch what kind of magic can happen. If therapists are interested in moving clients out of fixed problems states, sometimes they must perform out of the ordinary actions to move clients into more resourceful states. By creating new empowering experiences in the therapy setting, therapists can help their clients in taping into their own inner resources. These resources can alter patterns of emotion and behavior which clients previously felt helpless to change. The client's response can create openings for further creative investigations on the part of the therapist. As Keeney (1983) states, "The traditional view is that a therapist treats a client through a given intervention. However, it may be useful for a therapist to imagine a client's behavior as an intervention. His interventions, so to speak, attempt to provoke the therapist to come up with a useful directive or solution. In this reverse view the therapeutic behavior is problematic when he fails to help the client. Treatment is successful when the client provokes the therapist to say or prescribe the appropriate action" (p.19).

For a major change to take place in the therapy room, therapists need to make sure they are mobilizing aspects of the clients' emotional brain rather than just their logical, reasoning brain. The term "emotional brain" refers to the part of the brain which lies between the brain stem and the cerebral cortex. This part of the midbrain is involved in such processes as memory, motivation, learning and emotional feedback, and is activated by experience and solidified by repetition. If there is a desire to change a pattern located in the emotional part of the brain, then therapists must create a new experience in which those solidified patterns can be adjusted.

Armstrong (2015) emphasizes the importance of constructing therapy sessions in a way to facilitate activation of the emotional brain since the emotional brain comprehends through experience, repetition and sensory stimulation. Armstrong states, "The key is to create conditions that facilitate an experience that changes the implicit meaning and purpose associated with an emotional pattern. Furthermore, when you add an element of novelty, intrigue, humor or joy to the process of learning something new, the emotional brain really lights up and synthesizes new information in a deeper, more complete way" (p.13).

By becoming an active part of the therapy session, therapists will find it easier to create those unique experiences which facilitate activation of the emotional brain. Instead of habitual repetition of past interactions with clients, therapists should feel free to open up the therapy sessions to unexpected, spontaneous interventions creating an environment of novelty and healing. As Armstrong (2015) states, "You don't just want to have a compassionate conversation with your clients; you want to have an influential conversation that mobilizes them emotionally" (p.21).

I was working with a woman who had a history of being manipulated by her adult children, her ex-husband and anyone else she knew. She would do almost anything anyone asked of her, almost to the detriment of her life. She would not stand up for herself. She came to therapy because she desperately wanted things to be different. Even though she knew what her limiting beliefs were, she still continued her patterns of placating everyone. In our first session, she related how she felt helpless to change her familiar but dysfunctional patterns. She knew exactly why she did what she was doing, but she did not seem to be able to change. She knew she was seeking approval from others due to the history of her mother's neglect when she was a child. She knew that she needed to take back her own power and challenge her thinking patterns which told her she was not good enough, but she also told herself that the only way she could be considered worthwhile was if she martyred herself for others. She was a very intelligent and capable person, but she couldn't seem to alter her thinking.

In her second session with me, it was very clear to me that I could not depend on her conscious understanding of the situation to create any real change. She knew what the problem was, and yet still continued to create it. As she again began yet again to describe the injustices of all those people around her who continued to manipulate her, I immediately left the room leaving her in mid-sentence. Outside the door in the hallway there was a floor mat which I picked up and brought into the room with me. I closed the door behind me and then threw the mat on her lap. I then sat down and stared at her with no explanation. She looked at me with a shocked expression. We sat in silence for a little while she appeared to try and make sense of what had happened.

After a moment she began to cry. The mat slid off her lap onto the floor. I sat quietly while she cried. After a little while she began to stare at the mat as she cried. A minute later she pointed to it and said to me, "I don't want to be that." I nodded in approval. From that point on she began to talk about changing how she allows other people to treat her. A shift had occurred inside her that would not have happened until she had an experience which was out completely of the ordinary. She had to experience being a doormat in a way that activated her emotional brain. By having it experientially performed for her, she obtained something that cognitive restructuring alone could not accomplish.

From that point on, she began to interact differently with others. She began standing up for herself more often. She started setting boundaries where before she had had none. Gradually, she became more confident as she saw that people actually began to appreciate and respect her more when she set boundaries. This led her to become more self-assertive in many other areas of her life. It took an out of the ordinary experience of literally being a doormat to shift her thinking.

I have seen firsthand how creating novel experiences for clients can create substantial change in other areas of their lives when I had the immense pleasure of working with Dr. Linda Leech. Dr. Leech specializes in Equine Assisted Psychotherapy (EAP), which uses horses experientially for mental and behavioral therapeutic purposes. Clients in this form of therapy experience specific therapeutic interactions with horses which allow them to learn more about themselves and others. These interactions are then processed with the therapist and any new experiences with emotional and behavioral patterns are examined. Dr. Leech does much work with children and families who are dealing with everything from attention deficit disorders, Autism Spectrum disorders, obsessive compulsive disorder, post-traumatic stress disorder and parenting issues. She uses horses to indirectly assist her clients in discovering their own inner resources to effectively deal and triumph over their particular issues.

One thing I took away from watching and participating in these sessions is that little, if any, interpretation occurs. This kind of therapy is experiential and little insight is needed from the therapist. Observing the remarkable results of these sessions continues to solidify in my mind how we, as therapists, spend too much time focusing on etiology and not enough on guiding our clients in finding their own resources to heal. I clearly remember one example of a session I witnessed in which substantial change occurred after a short but effective experience.

A family sought help because of the five year old son's oppositional defiance and anxiety issues. The child's mother had divorced the child's father, and she and her child were now living with her new boyfriend. The boyfriend was very uncertain how to be a paternal influence for the child in this new situation. The boy had started rebelling against the boyfriend and not following the rules, therefore, wreaking havoc in the household. The mother appeared reluctant to take charge of the situation, and the boyfriend was very unsure of how to proceed in this relationship.

In their EAP session, this family was brought outside and placed in an enclosed area with three donkeys. They were instructed to find a way to keep each donkey away from each other. This proved to be a challenge since the donkeys, being social animals, really wanted to stay together and were very stubborn. The donkeys ran away from the family as a unit and were difficult to control in this situation. The mother and boyfriend began their task by asking the child to help them move the donkeys. Instead of assuming charge of the situation, they appeared to want the child to make the decisions about how best to begin their activity. The child was very confused and had no idea on how to complete the task. The mother was getting exasperated since she had no clue either. The boyfriend stayed quiet during most of the discussions about how to control the donkeys.

All of a sudden, Dr. Leech introduced another donkey into the enclosed area. She told the family that now they had to work with four donkeys instead of only three. At this point, the family was getting hot and tired under the beaming sun and had to do something. The mother walked off demonstrating that she did not want to make any decisions. It appeared that she wanted the child to make the decision on how to solve their problem. This apparently was a common behavior pattern at home. The mother seemed to give the boy too much responsibility in making decisions about things, and he responded in the natural way a child would respond. He created havoc due to his own anxiety about not knowing what to do.

Having walked to the side of the enclosed area, the mother appeared to have checked out of the activity. The boy began to get upset because he couldn't solve the problem. The mother began getting upset because her son was upset. The boyfriend stood quietly for about a minute. All of a sudden, the boyfriend took charge of the situation. He directed the mother and child as to the best way to separate all the donkeys. The boy listened to the boyfriend's directions and quickly took action with what he was told. The mother did the same. It was a struggle to reign in four independent minded donkeys, but the family was able to get the donkeys to separate to opposite sides of the enclosed area.

When the family came back to therapy a couple of weeks later, they said that things had improved a great deal at home. The boyfriend was taking a more active role within the household, and the mother was no longer running away from responsibility which had previously appeared to instigate the boy's emotional outbursts. The boy was acting out much less. When questioned about how this change happened, the family was not really sure, other than the boyfriend said that he somehow realized he needed to do more at home. All of these changes did not require one bit of conscious insight or interpretation during the therapy session. By actively creating a scenario in which the family had to adjust their regularly patterned behavior, the family found their own way to new behaviors without the need for in depth exploration of etiology.

Experiential aspects of the therapy process have been overshadowed for the last few years as much emphasis has been placed on more cognitive approaches. While cognitive approaches have much merit, sole focus on clients' thinking patterns often omits the crucial place that experience has in creating change. Armstrong states, "If you want to change a pattern stored at the level of the emotional brain….then you have to speak the non-verbal, sensory experiential language the emotional brain understands" (2015, p.11). Excessive searching for etiology and conscious comprehension can often limit the potential for change, as "insights and understanding happen as a result of experience not as a precursor to it" (Whitaker and Bumberry, 1988, p.86). If it took something out of the ordinary to knock clients off balance, then they may need something even more out of the ordinary to help them have the balance they seek.

Presupposition #4: Therapy is really about outcomes instead of origins

"Clients seek therapy not to review and analyze their lives but to transform them"

– Cloe Madanes

From the early beginnings of psychotherapy, there has been an effort to discover the cause of problems. Therapy was created by a desire to define, comprehend and diagnose the nature of humans. The early days of Freud centered on a systematic method of searching for and discovering the etiology of a client's issue. At that time, it was determined that etiology was due to unconscious conflicts. Later, a change in perspective moved the etiology toward a stimulus/response issue. In time the root causes of client problems became ideas such as conditions of worth, irrational thinking, existential angst, neurobiology, somatic processing, and so forth. All of these ideas about the origins of client problems may be absolutely true; however, ultimately none of these matter if the client is unable to change.

I have sensed a shift backwards in the practice of psychotherapy over the past few years. Often the field has become a static, empty process in which well-meaning therapists spend much of their time attempting to guide clients into obtaining insight and the understanding of the origins of their problems. This noble endeavor is a holdover from the days of Freud who believed that insight was crucial to therapeutic change. While insight is not necessarily a bad thing, I assert that it often has little to no bearing on whether clients change their life.

In spite of exciting new discoveries in the field over the

past several decades, in many cases therapy has gone backwards. Therapy has become a process in which therapists have clients go on a psychological archaeological expedition of their lives. These therapists hope that by having clients understand how and where their patterns of behavior originated, clients will obtain new insight that will stop their emotional pain. This occasionally may work, but more often it does not. Just because clients possess a solid account about the origin of their problem does not automatically create a positive therapeutic outcome. In their classic text, "The Tactics of Change: Doing Therapy Briefly", Fisch, Weakland and Seagal (1982) state, "Emphasis on hidden origins instead of what is presently observable necessarily leads to extensive inquiry about the past and to heavy use of inference. In addition, this view tends strongly, though often implicitly, toward viewing problems as the result of deficits in the individual's make up" (p.8).

If we want our clients to become transformed, then we, as therapists, must be transforming! We must motivate our clients to do something different rather than continue searching for causes. In the 1960s and 1970s amazing therapies (and therapists) emerged that shook the foundation of established past oriented approaches to change. The work of people such as Milton Erickson, Jay Haley, Virginia Satir, Salvador Minuchin, and many others gave the field a shot in the arm. There was life and creativity in their sessions, but with very little exploration of problem origin. These therapy masters obtained results by changing what their clients were doing, without spending excessive time exploring and interpreting clients' history.

How often have we had a session with a client who seemed to have a wonderful, life changing moment of insight into why he or she exhibits certain negative patterns only to find him or her two weeks later complaining of the same emotions, behaviors, or situations? It is far too common. Therapists must move away from solely encouraging insight and instead, begin to find creative ways clients can begin doing something new and different.   If the process of therapy is no different from what clients are already experiencing, then what is the point of coming to a therapy session?

Spending most of a session focused on deterministically finding the origin of problems moves one further away from being aware if the client's desired outcomes are being met. A single minded quest for a cure based on a deep understanding of the etiology of the problem can limit creativity and flexibility on the part of the clinician. As Freedman states, "As psychotherapists, we often become enamored with theories and explanations. At times, this search for explanations leads us into a more complex jungle of ideas and hypothesizing, immerses us in an interminable morass of blame and dysfunction" (1994, p.218). The desire of client understanding as a curative can be dubious, as Cozolino states, "In psychotherapy, understanding is the booby prize. It is a hollow victory to end up with a detailed psychological explanation for problems that remain unchanged" (2004, p.34).

Many of us entered the field of psychotherapy trained to find solutions to client problems through a strict linear cause and effect perspective. As Boscolo and Betrando state, "many therapists, especially those with medical training, tend to look for the underlying causes - i.e. the "real" causes – of the pathology. They get involved in a search that, due to the current lack of knowledge, may well turn out to be all in vain. It may even be dangerous because it tends to freeze attention on the "illness" to the detriment of what may be seen as "normal or "healthy"" (p.47).

By committing ourselves solely to a theory which primarily

focuses on seeking explanations as to "why" clients respond a certain way in their lives instead of "how" they can change, therapists run the risk of missing the possibilities for methods to aid the alleviation of suffering. As Corbett (2011) states, "Commitment to a theory may make us too confident that we understand what is going on. Theory then acts to prevent change. Anything that is fixed becomes mechanical, and there is a risk that the accumulation of theory and technique that we impose in our training may produce a restricted image of the person or a routine that may prevent the therapist from seeing what is actually happening" (p.45).

Presupposition #5: Direct clients toward the future

**"Action must happen if change is to happen.
Nondirective therapy is actionless"**

– Jay Haley

Many years ago much of the focus of therapy was on the past history of clients. The therapist first thoroughly investigated what had happened to clients during crucial developmental periods of their lives. After that, there was repeated in depth discussions on how clients felt about what happened to them. It was proposed that if clients were worked with in this manner they would be better equipped to deal with the day to day challenges of the present. Therapists believed it was difficult for clients to have productive, happy lives if they were weighed down by what Fritz Perls referred to as "unfinished business."

In spite of exciting new discoveries in the field over the past several decades, often therapy has gone backwards and become a process where therapists have clients become focused on their past. I hope that one of the next trends in psychotherapy will be to, instead of only a past or present orientation, clients will be guided toward a future orientation. It is in the future that change can occurs. The past is over and cannot be changed. Understanding what could happen in the future helps clients to create a new lives. I believe in the importance of clients having what O'Hanlon (2014) calls a "future pull", a purpose or a task that motivates and energizes them to begin the process of change and growth.

If therapists are solely focused on the past history of their clients, an important part of the change process may be missed. If clients do not recognize all the positive possibilities for the future, then it is no wonder they feel stuck and unable to get past their "past." Too often therapists focus their attention (and indirectly the client's attention) on what had not worked in the past. Repeated in depth explorations of the past does little to "pull" clients into a more resourceful state of relating to their issues. When the client has motivation or inspiration to focus on the future, it speeds up the healing process as clients can now move beyond feeling stuck in the past or present.

No matter what style of therapy one does, having a "future pull" can be adopted into almost any session. It is important to respect our clients' pasts, but at the same time, we must also assist them in finding the inner resources they need to guide them toward a positive future of their own creation. For therapy to be alive there has to be movement. Even though we want to honor our clients' life stories, we must also balance that with explorations of what "could be" rather than "what was." Clients should be directed toward future outcomes which are inspiring and empowering. The therapist will need to become a director of the session, rather than the passive observer of what transpires. The more we emphasize the future utilization of resources in our sessions, the greater the likelihood of shifting our clients' perspective from the feeling that they are stuck in a problem to exploring ways out of the problem. As Furman and Ahola (1994) suggest, "The single most useful issue to be talked about with clients is how they view the future without the problem......When people are helped to foresee a good future for themselves, they automatically begin to view their present difficulties as a transitory phase, rather than as an everlasting predicament" (p.55).

The future we help our clients to envision must be a compelling future. If the future is not compelling and inspiring, then it is unlikely that clients will see it through. I have found this to be very true when working with clients who are in the recovery phase of addiction. If a future without the addictive substance is not at least as enthralling as their past lifestyle, then it may be more difficult to maintain their sobriety. When people are captivated by the possibility of something wonderful happening in the future, they are be more open to exploring options other than their previous behavioral patterns. By shifting clients' focus toward something exciting and enticing, we are helping to open up the frame of what they consider possible about themselves.

Dan came to therapy because of his drinking problem, and had just come out of a twenty eight day treatment program. He was grappling with how to approach the world without his previous patterns of soothing his anxiety through alcohol. He said that he was committed to staying sober, and I was sure that he believed this was true. However, I noticed that other than attending Alcoholic Anonymous meetings and working at his job, Dan had no other activities in his life that motivated him. This lack of enthusiasm for life in general could eventually lead back to the familiar pattern of drowning his sorrows with alcohol. Dan had done well in his recovery program and was following the after-care treatment guidelines of the program, but there was nothing that motivated him to feel differently about his life.

I asked Dan what inspired him. He replied that he was not sure, because his focus now was on getting back to work and fulfilling all financial and familial duties required of him. I complimented him on his dedication to following through on his responsibilities. I continued to ask him what was inspiring to him until he finally told me that he had always wanted to go into the field of marine biology. He laughed as he said it as if he did not feel he could ever do what he had really wanted to do. I asked him how he could make that a reality within the next few years. Dan looked at me as if I had asked him to defy the law of gravity. He told me that there was absolutely no way he could become a marine biologist. He gave me a multitude of reasons why work and family responsibilities would keep him from returning to college to pursue his dream. At the same time he was telling me why he could not do what he had dreamed, I could tell that a part of Dan had suddenly awoken. I could see that the part of him that wanted to be a marine biologist had been slumbering for a long time.

After spending a little time listening to and playfully challenging his objections to pursuing his dream, I asked Dan if he would do one thing for me before the next session. He should contact the local college to obtain some information about their biology program. He would not have to sign up for anything or commit to returning to school. He only had to bring proof that he had spoken to someone about the program as a sign of good faith. He hesitantly agreed to the therapeutic task, but he made sure again that I understood it would not be easy for him to go back to school.

The next session Dan came in with a handful of brochures and business cards from different people he had spoken with at the college. He appeared excited as he spoke about what happened during his therapeutic task. He told me how comfortable he had felt going back onto a college campus and how surprised he was that the people he spoke with were very enthusiastic about giving him information about marine biology. Dan admitted that he had always felt a little embarrassed about telling anyone that he wanted to go into the field since some of his family members had said less than flattering things about the income potential for marine biologists. Dan found the enrollment counselors and professors showed interest in him and his dream which he found to be both comforting and affirming. He also told me that going to college part time was something that he could do even with a busy schedule since courses meet both in class and online. Dan had found a "future pull" that did not involve alcohol.

In future sessions Dan reported back the steps he was taking to, not only maintain his sobriety, but also to work toward his long term goal of becoming a marine biologist. He researched where graduate programs were located and how he could transfer with his present job when the time came for him to move away to study. Dan found that he was more energetic and alive with his long term goal, and for once in a very long time, he was feeling inspired. His enthusiasm was contagious and I looked forward to our sessions so that I could hear about the next big step he had taken toward his dream. I honestly believe that if Dan had not found an inspiring future for himself, he would have eventually ended back in the grip of addiction.

Since many of us have treatment plans and outcome measures, why not add an inspiring future along with the usual goals of therapy? The absence of a symptom does not always mean that transformation has taken place. Find out what really motivates your clients and use those resources to open up new possibilities for them. Make a compelling, inspiring future a necessary component of a treatment plan and notice what is different in how you approach your therapy sessions. You may find that your clients' futures are brighter than you, and they, remotely imagined them to be.

CHAPTER 3: THE RELUCTANT PREACHER

Even in some of the toughest cases we can look for resources which clients can utilize. It can be difficult when a therapist gets a case which seems so bad that he or she feels stuck inside the context of the problem. It is important to stay focused and creative when working with emotionally difficult cases as there are usually resources available, but, due to the nature of the situation, these resources are easily obscured by the emotional content.

Maggie and Anthony came to therapy seeking help in dealing with their son's suicide which had happened three weeks earlier. When I went to the waiting room to bring them back for their session I did not know the reason for their seeking therapy. Both were dressed shabbily and looked as if they had not slept well in a while. Maggie was polite but was very stoic in her mannerisms while Anthony came across as a very gentle person with one of the saddest smiles I can remember seeing.

They sat down in the therapy room and I asked what brought them in. They both immediately began weeping uncontrollably. Maggie told me her son, Michael, had committed suicide right in front of them. She described how she and Anthony had gone to see their son at his home and found him attacking his wife and children. After they physically became involved in the struggle between Michael and his family, Maggie and Anthony successfully removed Michael's wife and daughter from the home and went back inside to check on Michael. As soon as they came back into the house, Michael ran to the bedroom and then returned with a firearm. They believed he was going outside to shoot his wife, but instead Michael put the gun in his mouth and pulled the trigger. They both witnessed his suicide and desperately attempted to save him. Michael died within a few moments of shooting himself as he lay in his mother's arms.

This horrific ordeal had devastated Maggie and Anthony. Their intense releasing of grief in my office may have been one of the first times they had allowed themselves to feel the full weight of what happened since the day Michael had killed himself. Both struggled to tell their story but after a minute of their struggle to talk while sobbing I told them to not worry about speaking and to take all the time they needed to allow their emotions to flow. In several years of doing therapy this was one of the most intense expressions of grief and pain I had witnessed. To say that these people were emotionally devastated would be an understatement.

M: Maggie

A: Anthony

T: Therapist

T: I am so very sorry for your loss. There are no words that can adequately comfort you when something like this has happened.

M: He was my baby boy, and I can't believe he is gone. (sobbing)

A: I tried to get to him when I saw the gun, but I couldn't. (sobbing)

T: There was nothing you could have done.

M: He always had emotional problems, but I never thought he

would want to hurt his family or kill himself. He could be so sweet sometimes. I just don't know why.

A: I feel like there is a hole inside me that can't be filled. All I can remember is seeing the back of his head when he pulled that trigger.....why...WHY? (Anthony has grown more intense in his speech, but stops abruptly as he is overcome with emotion and sits quietly as he cries)

At this point the most important thing to do was to give these parents a place to let out any emotions they were experiencing. Attempting to do any intervention so soon would not only be ineffective, but would also dishonor their trust by not allowing them to feel their grief.

M: We can't get the image of him with that gun out of our minds. I don't think either of us has slept since it happened. I am worried about Anthony as he isn't eating enough.

A: I am worried about you, too. You aren't eating or sleeping either. If I do go to sleep I dream about what happened. I end up waking up many times throughout the night wondering if all of it really happened.

M: I do too. I think about holding Michael in my arms when he was a baby....and I think about him not being here...I don't know anymore. (crying)

A: I don't understand it at all.

T: You mentioned Michael had emotional problems. Was he violent before this incident happened?

M: No. He would get really angry and kick or punch the walls, but he wouldn't hit anyone. I was shocked when I walked in and saw him strangling his wife that day. I don't know what would have happened if we hadn't showed up when we did.

A: He would have killed them! He would have killed both of them! He loved his daughter so much, but he was just unhinged that day. They were scared of him, but he hadn't attacked them before that day. He was such a loving person, but he could be so angry at times. He would lose touch with reality and think everyone was out to get him. But he could be such a sweet boy….now he is gone.

Maggie holds Anthony's hand as he collapses against her into an embrace which almost resembles a child clinging to his mother. Maggie has returned to a stoic presence as she appears to have shifted her emotional state to be strong for Anthony. I suspect that she is usually the strong one and the leader in the relationship and is possibly not giving herself the opportunity to grieve outside of this therapy session.

T: If this was a case of mental illness, which is what it certainly sounds like, I want you to know that Michael might not have been able to understand what was really going on. His perception may have been clouded by issues within his brain. If he loved his family as you say, then this certainly may have been something out of anyone's ability to control.

A: I just don't think he would have done any of this if he had been in his right mind.

T: Right, sometimes these things happen due to problems of a biological nature. I don't know the case in this situation, but it may be that Michael was reacting in a way that made sense to him due to some chemical issues of which none of us could possibly be aware.

I want to offer alternative explanations for Michael's behavior so that Maggie and Anthony are not stuck in a self-blaming cycle as there appears to be little to nothing they could have done to prevent Michael's behavior.

M: He never would have hurt anyone most of the time. It was like he lost touch with reality.

A: Yeah, he wasn't Michael when he was that way. He became something else, but it didn't happen that often. He could be so helpful to people.

T: Yes, when these things happen it is like the person involved can't tell what is really happening. It sounds like you are two brave people to jump in and help Michael's wife and daughter like that.

M: We couldn't let him hurt or possibly kill them. He wasn't in his right mind....he really loved his daughter. Now she doesn't have a father.....

Maggie begins sobbing again, and we all sit quietly for a full minute or two to allow her the space to let her emotions out. Anthony puts his arm on her shoulder for support as she cries.

A: We don't know how one moves on after this kind of thing. I still think he is alive sometimes. It seems like it is a bad dream that I can't seem to wake up from, and I really want to wake up. I catch myself expecting him to call me like he used to, and then I feel even worse when I realize he won't ever call me again.

M: I can't get those images out of my head. I just want to go to sleep and wake up to find everything the way it was.

T: I can understand that. I have to be honest and tell you that this is one of the worst things a person can go through and is the worst thing a parent can go through. I want you to know that everything that you are feeling is a normal reaction to what has happened to you. Not only have you lost a child, you had to witness his death. I am so surprised that you both are doing as well as you are.

M: Well, I don't feel like I am doing well at all.

T: I understand

A: Other people can't seem to understand what it is like.

M: I have Michael's picture on my cell phone and some people are telling me that is not good for me.

Maggie shows me her cell phone which has a photo of Michael on the screen.

T: Who told you it was not good for you?

M: Other people in the family.

T: I have to respectfully disagree with them. I think it is important during this time for you to honor your son's memory.

A: We talk about him all the time. Every day at 5:30 in the afternoon, we both just break down.

T: Why 5:30?

M: That is when he died.

T: Oh.

A: When that clock hits 5:30 we both start to get really upset. I hate when that time rolls around. The only thing I can think to do is say a prayer.

T: Are you both religious?

Here I am seeking a resource which both can begin to reorganize their experiences around.

M: Yes, very. Some folks want us to be angry at God, but we aren't. God helps us get through the day. It wasn't God's fault so we don't blame him at all.

A: God is what pulls me through the day. As hard as it is I can't imagine how I would deal with all this without God.

T: So your faith is a great comfort to you?

A: Yes sir.

T: That is wonderful.

M: Throughout my life God has helped me, and I don't think he will stop helping me now.

T: Anthony, you told me that when 5:30 rolls around you have to say a prayer because of all the pain you and Maggie are feeling. Do you say it out loud?

A: Yes.

T: Would you say the prayer now for me?

Anthony smiles in a shy way and thinks for a second.

A: Dear Lord, help us to understand why things happen and enlighten us to your divine plan. Give us the strength to accept what has happened…..and allow us to move past the pain of this situation. We love you…… and we want to follow your path. Please keep us safe and help us heal our hearts. In Jesus' name, Amen.

T: Wow. That was really good. (To Maggie) Did you hear the power he had in his voice?

M: Yes.

T: Does hearing that prayer give you comfort?

M: Absolutely

T: (To Anthony) Have you ever thought of becoming a preacher?

Instantly the energy in the room changes as both Anthony and Maggie look very surprised and both begin to cry.

M: He always wanted to be a preacher.

T: Well, you would make a great one based on the prayer I just heard.

A: I never thought I could do something like that. I do want to share the Lord's word with others, but I never really thought I could do it.

T: Why not?

With Anthony's desire to preach now known, there is way out of the frame of the problem. By shifting the direction of the session toward Anthony's desire to preach the pathway to new resources for Anthony and Maggie begins to open up.

A: I never thought there was anything special about me. I have heard some great preachers speak and they always seemed to have a special calling that I don't have.

T: Maybe this is your calling?

A: How so?

T: Maybe what you do with this terrible thing that has happened with Michael is a calling? There are many people out there in the world who go through this kind of thing, too many people. Having someone who can speak to them who has been there and still loves God and wants to share his message could be a real gift.

M: He always is the one to say the blessing at the meals. He is so very devoted to the Lord.

T: Right. Maybe your calling is hidden in this tragedy.

At this point both Anthony and Maggie are exhibiting a shift in their mood. They appear very attentive and surprised.

A: I always wanted to share the Gospel with others. I was just afraid that no one would take me seriously.

T: You are now a man who has been through one of the worst things a person can go through and, yet, you still love God. If people don't take that seriously, then I don't know if they can take anything seriously!

M: That's true.

T: I think both of you have a remarkable message to share with others. No matter what you have gone through you both still don't blame God. You both still love God and want to share the Gospel with others. Wow. You know, just sitting here with both of you gives me the feeling that you two are supposed to be working together in some special kind of way.

A: What do you mean?

T: What I mean is that it feels to me that you two are supposed to be doing something powerful from this point on.

A: Do you mean spiritually?

T: It could be. I was really surprised how quickly you came up with that special prayer and how much authority you had in your voice when you said it.

A: I don't know. I'm real reluctant to do any kind of preaching even though part of me wants to do it. I guess I'm scared…

T: I understand because it is a big mission to go out and share your story with others.

A: Yeah....I'm just reluctant.

T: Yes, you are the reluctant preacher. That is so great.

A: Huh?

M: How is that great?

T: I mean that he is so humble. There are so many people out there who want to jump up and be preachers because they want the power, or they want the fame. Anthony is a reluctant preacher because he doesn't want to do it for the wrong reasons. He doesn't want to be one of those guys who wants to be a preacher because he can be a big shot or make a lot of money. He is a reluctant preacher, and that is so honest and deeply spiritual to me.

M: It is. He is very humble. (To Anthony) You know you do very well when you have to pray in front of everyone. You do a good job.

A: I like to lead the prayers, but I don't know if I could really be a preacher. I have always wanted to share the Word of God with others, but I didn't know if I could.

T: You see, that is the humility I love to hear. He is not sure because he knows what an important message he has and he wants to do it right.

The direction of therapy has shifted away from Michael's death to Anthony's humility and call to preach. This is opening up a pathway to inner resources for both Maggie and Anthony. By being open to becoming more involved in preaching and discussing spiritual matters it gives both of them access to their resource of faith. This can be of immense value to them through this extraordinarily difficult time.

A: I do want to help others. I want to help others who have been though the kind of thing we have.

T: I think that is wonderful. I also wonder if this is a mission for both of you.

Maggie and Anthony both sit quietly for a few moments processing my comment.

A: It may be.

M: I want to help others as well. God has helped me so much in the past that I want to share his message of love with others. I think there are many people who have lost their faith after going through what we have, but we both haven't. We both feel even stronger in our faith.

A: It's true. I hear about people who lose their faith when they have something really bad happen to them, but that is the time to move closer to God, not away from him.

T: When I hear both of you speak about your faith I hear a lot of authority in both your voices. I hear a message that other people might want to hear. (To Anthony) I know up until this point you have been reluctant to begin preaching, but you don't have to go out and start a church right away. Maybe all you need to do is to start doing some preaching at home with the family and maybe a few friends? I think this whole family might need to hear your message.

M: Yes.

A: I guess I could.

T: It just popped into my mind what I want you to do for the next week. I want you both to do a special thing for me every day over the next seven days. I want you to go buy a white candle. Pick out any large candle that really appeals to you. I want both of you and any other friends or family members who are around at that time to gather around and light that candle at 5:30 and have Anthony say a special prayer of healing. Every day a different prayer needs to be said. A prayer of healing for all people involved in this tragedy. I also think you should ask for strength and direction in pursuing your mission to share your story and help others. I think you should do this every day for the next week.

Both Maggie and Anthony begin to cry again.

M: That is so beautiful.

A: Yes, I will do it. Thank you.

T: Yeah, every day for the next seven days.

A: Ok.

T: And feel free to invite other family members and friends to this ceremony. They may need to hear your prayer as well. They also probably feel a real sense of loss and need to feel uplifted.

M: They do.

A: Michael's wife and daughter are still in shock. His friends have called and some have stopped by the house to check on us.

T: That is great that so many people want to check on both of you. You two have such a wonderful partnership that others want to be close to and make sure you are all right.

A: Yes, so many folks have been nice and helpful to us.

T: Light that candle and say those prayers, ok?

A: Yes.

M: We will.

When following up with Anthony and Maggie, they both detailed how they had followed the directive to light the candle and have Anthony pray every day for a week at 5:30pm. Various members of the family came by to take part in the ceremony as well as several friends. After the first week it was decided to move the ceremony to 6:30pm so that more people could take part in the ceremony since most people did not get off work in time to get there. By the end of the second week there had been an increase in the number of people attending, and the topic of the prayer sessions had shifted into areas not limited to just Michael's passing. Both Anthony and Maggie were discussing religious ideas with those who attended the ceremony. By the time they came back to therapy it had been decided that there would be a once a week gathering at Anthony and Maggie's home which would be called "Michael's Hour" in memory of their son. The focus of the hour would be discussion of how to apply God's wisdom in one's life during troubling times.

Anthony appeared more confident in how he was interacting with others, and Maggie appeared to look less stoic. Even though they still grieved the loss of their son, there seemed to be an acceptance of his death with a new focus on helping others who have experienced loss. Anthony still feels he is not up to being a preacher, but he states maybe God knows best. Maggie feels a renewed sense of partnership with Anthony and is becoming more comfortable experiencing her own emotions of grief and loss. She remarked how inspired she has been by Anthony's prayers and lectures.

 Even in difficult cases it is important for therapists to look for and utilize resources to facilitate healing.

.

CHAPTER 4: FINDING RESOURCES

In moving away from problem investigation and moving toward resource activation, it is crucial to find the necessary resources within our clients. Even in some of the toughest cases, we can find some resource which can help our clients to move forward in their lives and overcome what they perceive as mental and emotional limitations. Having flexibility in our search for resources is very important since often clients, as they experience hardship, do not believe that they have any resources at their disposal.

To successfully discover and then implement necessary resources in therapy sessions, therapists must step out of the "problem frame" of the initial interaction with clients and begin to search for the clients' emotions, actions or beliefs which can accelerate healing. Once therapists become resource directed, they may find the therapy process becomes more enjoyable and effective. Their clients will sometimes make surprising shifts in how they feel and what actions they take. To quote Furman and Ahola (1994), "Everyone has some resource, such as skills, capabilities, talents, interests, admirable character traits, and so forth that can be utilized in solving the problem. However, these resources may go unnoticed unless the therapist deliberately focuses on finding out about them. A person with a good sense of humor can be coached to use his wit and humor in solving his problem; another person who is skillful in writing can be helped to take advantage of that skill" (p.49).

Anything and everything has the potential to be a resource for clients. Even some things considered negative could contain resourceful applications. Anger may be used as a resource in motivating a person to make changes in how he or she approaches his or her problem. Confusion may become a catalyst to understanding. Even anxiety can be applied in the proper context. Carl Whitaker who utilized a families' anxiety to create the necessary change commented on his own work, "I do not want to relieve their anxiety. I want their anxiety to be the power that makes things move. Then I want to combine with it to make the anxiety more productive" (Whitaker & Bumberry, 1988, p. 11). Resources that seem to get the most results are usually positive resources, however, we do not want to discount any possibility based on our own preconceived judgments.

The easiest way I have found in teaching therapists to find resources is through the acronym "**V.I.B.E.S**". This acronym stands for the following: **Values, Identity, Behaviors, Environment** and **Spirituality**. Each of these areas is an excellent place to begin looking for resources. We can find resources in one or all of these areas and help our clients to make changes in how they relate to their problems. When they discover they have a resource, often change begins to happen in unexpected ways. We will examine each of these V.I.B.E.S. with examples to see how they can be used to help our clients. Resources are not compartmentalized in only one area of a person's life. If we access a resource in one area, then that same resource may be utilized in other areas.

VALUES

Values are the priorities, activities, and the beliefs associated with them that guide our lives. Each individual has his or her own unique set of values which dictates the direction he or she takes in life. When we focus on our highest values, we have a sense of fulfillment and competence. Our values give us hope and meaning in our lives. If we become disengaged from our highest values, we often fall into emotional distress and existential angst. According to Demartini (2013), "Your highest values may change throughout your life – most people's do – but they are still the very essence of you: what you're drawn to, what you inevitably seek out, what you live for. They are a kind of internal compass, pointing you toward the activities, people, and places that most fulfill you and away from the situations and people that are likely to feel unfulfilling. If you think of which activities, and relationships truly nourish your innermost being, those are your highest values" (p.12).

Often when we attempt to place priority on someone else's values instead of our own, we become frustrated and lack satisfaction when we achieve the goals associated with those misplaced values. In some cases, our clients have gone through an experience which has caused them to lose touch with their own values. Part of our job may be to help clients to rediscover their inner most values and to align themselves with those values. In realigning to their own values, clients often gain energy, focus and satisfaction in areas of their lives once considered barren.

For example, imagine a man has as his highest value spending time with his family. In spite of this value, he also feels the need to be economically prosperous. Because he wants to be secure economically, he finds a good paying job which unfortunately requires him to be away from his family for extended periods of time. Consciously, he thinks he is being a good provider for his family, but unconsciously he has assumed societal expectations about increasing his earning potential. This may not be in alignment with his higher value of spending time with his family. The increased income is very nice; however, he finds a growing discontent with his life because of his disengagement with his family. His excessive focus on his work has caused a shifting away from his highest value of spending time with his family. He tries to focus more on his work, telling himself that he does not need to worry about spending time with family as it is more important at this stage of his life to pursue career and financial opportunities.

Over time, he finds himself suffering from the symptoms of depression. He is unaware of why he is feeling this way, but his moving away from his personal values has created a despairing emotional state. In order to decrease his feelings of despair, it is important for him to access the resource of his highest value: his family. By interacting with his family more often, he finds that his feelings of despair lessen. This may even cause him to question whether he really wants to stay on the emotional treadmill created by his career or whether he needs to reevaluate his decisions about his future.

We are often unaware of our own values. We unconsciously operate with them. Often we are surprised at how much easier our lives can become when we acknowledge our highest values and adjust our lives accordingly. It is as if, "your highest values determine your attention, retention, and intention: what you notice, what you remember, and what you intend or act upon" (Demartini, 2013, p.19). The more we take actions which do not line up with our values, the more we feel tired, uncertain, and disappointed in our lives. If we make a conscious choice to act on our values more often, we give ourselves access to resources which will direct our lives into more positive directions.

When we work with our clients, we need to ask them about the things they value the most. Clients will often just say things which are socially acceptable, but have little real emotional connection to them. By asking what truly inspires them or what they really enjoy doing, we begin to access the resources for healing which lay dormant. By just discussing things which give clients a feeling of connection to themselves, we activate resources useful to all areas of their lives.

I once worked with a woman named Julia who had sought therapy because of her depression and lack of motivation in her work. Julia was a manager in a large, thriving company, but she reported she felt unable to focus on her work. Julia showed signs of vocational and emotional burnout. She said she felt stuck in her life and wanted to begin enjoying life again. She was exasperated because she did not understand what was "wrong" with her. It became apparent that her desire to make her job her highest value was not working for her.

When I asked Julia what activity she really had enjoyed in her life and what brought her a feeling inspiration, it did not take long for her to tell me that one of her greatest loves in life was dancing. She described how she had danced since she was a child and her extensive experience competing in dance competitions. When Julia no longer performed competitively, she began teaching at a local dance school. As she talked about her interest in dancing, I noticed an immediate shift in her physical posture. She appeared much more energetic and more enthusiastic than when she had entered the therapy room earlier.

When I asked her when the last time she had danced, she said that it had been a long time. She told me how she had become involved in her work and had let the dancing go. I noticed that when she discussed her work, her body slumped and she adopted a depressed posture. The problem was that her highest value was dancing and teaching dance, not being a manager at a large company. Julia was not honoring her highest value and instead she was focusing too much of her mental energy on an activity that did not inspire her.

I directed Julia to begin buying some magazines about dancing and then cut out inspiring pictures of dancing. She was then to use the pictures to make a collage dedicated to dance. I suggested she spend some time every day sitting with the poster she had created reflecting on what was missing in her life. When she returned to therapy a few weeks later, Julia stated that she had followed the directive and had become aware that she was not dancing anywhere in her life. She began dancing alone at home and found that she enjoyed the simple act of moving around to music. She then called a local dance group which participated in dance competitions and volunteered her services. When the dance group learned of Julia's background, they quickly asked if she would be a judge at the next regional competition.

Julia later told me that she now felt more focused at her work and had more energy. She now saw her job as a means to fund her excursions into the world of dance, which made the job much more enjoyable. By reconnecting with her highest value, Julia felt a renewed sense of contentment that she had not found in her work. In time, she discovered that she could dedicate even more time to activities related to dance and provide herself with a greater sense of purpose in her life.

IDENTITY

How we identify ourselves provides a mindset that either empowers us or creates emotional hardship. People identify themselves with areas such as religious affiliation, a particular sports team, their birth order in the family, political leanings, type of employment, hobbies, and choice of entertainment, to name a few. Among all of these ways clients may identify themselves, lie resources that therapists can utilize to move clients outside the frame of their problem.

Asking our clients how they see themselves can yield important information about what direction to take in therapy. If a client has identified herself as a "caregiver", a "teacher", or a "warrior", then each one of these identities can be potential strengths the client can use to overcome her particular issue. If the client's identity is that of a "caregiver", then she could be directed to consider giving more of her time toward a good cause. This will create more social interactions for her, as well as, feelings of accomplishment. If the identity is "teacher", then she could discover new ways to learn and then share what she has learned with others, giving her a feeling of mastery. If she envisions herself as a "warrior", then she can use her willingness to fight to create new outcome in her own situation.

Unfortunately, I have found that the people who have the most trouble changing their lives are often the ones who have most identified with their "problem". Unconsciously they think that if they change, they will cease to be who they are. When clients have taken on the identity of their issue, it is difficult for them to understand that their lives could be different. Consciously, clients may want to be different, but unconsciously they are limited in options. Their sense of identity is invested in "the problem". Continued problem investigation and focus in therapy will often cause the client's identity as "the problem" to be solidified.

Andy came to therapy when his life fell apart after the death of his wife. He had a small one person business in which he installed, repaired, and replaced windows in houses. He had worked very hard over the years to provide a nice home for his wife, who had suffered from a medical condition which caused her extreme amounts of pain. She had unexpectedly died due to complications in her medical condition. Andy was in shock. As a result of his being blindsided by the death of his spouse, Andy had begun spiraling into a deep depression. He stopped working and ended up losing his business. As a result of losing his business, he had to move in with his aging parents due to his financial problems, and he found himself less and less motivated to do anything different. Andy was stuck in depression, and reluctantly, at the insistence of his parents, he came to therapy to get help.

After spending some time determining what was going on with Andy, I realized that not only had he lost his beloved wife, but he lost his identity as well. He had identified himself so much with his business that he felt there was nowhere for him to find solace with both his wife and business gone. Rather than addressing the intense grief he felt about his wife's death, it was better, in the short term, to get him back some of his identity. I told him that the most important thing we needed to do was to get him back into a business. I let him know that, even though I was terribly sorry to hear about his wife's death, it was of the greatest importance to launch his business return to the community.

Andy appeared surprised to hear that I advocated launching back into a business. We began to discuss the steps it would take for him to open a new business and do what he loved. We broke each step down into more manageable smaller steps to take over the next two weeks. His demeanor changed in the session when he saw that all was not lost when it came to his identity as a business owner. He became emotional when I asked if he would like to change the name of his business to reflect a new era of his life. I even wonder aloud if perhaps he could name his new business after his departed spouse. He became more energetic as the session progressed, and we planned to talk briefly over the phone in a week to check his progress.

Within a week, I spoke with Andy, and he sounded like a different man. He had begun following the plan we had set up for starting his business, but he was far ahead of schedule and had already taken most of the actions required. Andy sounded more self-assured and focused as he described his latest business activity. Starting a new business gave him a reason to get out of bed in the morning, and since this business would be a tribute to his deceased wife, he wanted to make sure everything went as it should. He felt it would dishonor her memory if he didn't get up and take charge of his business. I repeatedly told him how amazed I was that he was back in business so soon. Since Andy had taken back his identity as a "business man", he had more energy and drive to move forward. He was also moving toward a better place emotionally so that he would eventually begin working through the grief he had with the loss his wife.

BEHAVIORS

Each person has achieved success somewhere in his or her life. When clients are in the midst of turmoil; however, it is very easy for them to forget that they are capable of remarkable behavior which lead to success. By reintroducing clients to those behaviors or by suggesting new behaviors, clients can then begin to have success in other areas of their lives. Again, resources do not have to be compartmentalized into one area of life. If the client has confidence in one area of life, then it is much easier for that confidence to seep over into other areas. Utilizing and altering client behaviors in a manner which helps them to access personal strengths is the most fundamental action in a resource directed approach to helping people change.

Questioning our clients about their past achievements can open up those resources to application in a different context. By asking clients how they have successfully overcome hardship in the past creates within them an experience of successful coping which could be applied to the present problem they are encountering. Being reminded of what actions one took to change a situation from the past may be all that is needed for clients to reactivate those same behaviors in the present and future. The past actions taken that centered on client strengths should be fully investigated and utilized in approaching future obstacles.

Sam sought therapy to deal with his anxiety and depression. He had been depressed for close to a year and he traced the onset of his anxious feeling to almost four years ago when he was still living in a large city. Since that time he had moved away from the city to where he grew up, a very small town with little cultural activities. He also had broken up with a long-time girlfriend before he moved back to his hometown. Since his move, he had been unable to find work and thus felt isolated and had little contact with friends. He felt helpless to change anything in his life.

Sam wanted his confidence back. I assured him that that was a good goal to work toward. I asked him what he would actions he would need to take in order to get his confidence back. He replied that he didn't know. He didn't think he could ever feel confident again. I assured him that, although he may feel like that in the moment, I was sure he could find new ways to be confident in the future. However, in order to feel confident he needed to be doing something that gave him confidence. Immediately Sam dismissed what I was saying. He told me that he didn't believe he could ever do anything that would give him confidence since he didn't feel confident. Although I understood his thinking, I said that, even though confidence is a feeling, it is a feeling based on how one thinks and acts. My recommendation was to find things in his life which he could do to bring back his confidence. Sam was very hesitant to even think about doing anything different with his life.

After a few minutes of struggling to get him to consider doing something different, I realized that Sam was in full "pity party" mode. He believed that his situation was the worst thing on the planet, and he didn't believe that anything that he did would change anything. He acted as if everything in his entire life was bad and would not even consider that there were any positive experiences in his life over the past couple of years. He truly believed that he was stuck where he was and did not want to do anything about it. He was depressed, and he decided he was defeated. Any attempt to pull him out was futile at this point.

Cognizant that anything I directly tried would be shot down by Sam, I continued asking him about his daily routine. I asked him about his diet and exercise. He told me that his diet wasn't great and that he used to exercise but didn't feel like exercising anymore. I suggested that he might feel better if he took regular walks or went to the gym. He immediately shot down all my suggestions, but then he told me something that jumped out to me as a resource. He told me that, after several years of smoking cigarettes, he had decided to stop smoking two years ago. His admission to a success was what was needed to activate a much needed resource within him.

I told Sam how impressed I was that he was able to stop an

addiction that seemed to plague so many people. I told him that many people find it nearly impossible to stop smoking since nicotine was one of the most addictive substances. I then asked him how specifically he had gained the "confidence" to quit smoking. I wanted to know what steps he took to "create such a change" in his life. Sam thought for a moment and then said, "I had to get in the right mindset. I had to know that I could change even though it would be difficult. I just thought about what my life would be like if I didn't change, and that gave me the motivation to do what I wanted. It wasn't easy but I made myself do it."

At this point in our conversation I noticed a major shift in Sam's speech and his posture. Previously he slumped over while detailing his pity party and breathed very shallow. As he began to tell how he triumphed over his nicotine addiction, he sat up a little straighter, spoke with more authority, and was breathing much more deeply. Just by talking about his accomplishment caused a small shift in him that appeared to be that mysterious feeling of confidence he was sought. By just thinking of a time when he felt confident and could follow through on a goal, Sam activated those resources lying dormant as he wallowed in self-pity.

Using the guise of wanting to know more about how someone could successfully stop smoking so that I could help other clients who struggled with smoking, I continued asking him specific questions about his successful smoking cessation skills. I wanted to hear from him, in detail, how he continued to be confident enough to stay smoke free after a many years of smoking. My goal was to continue eliciting these feelings from within Sam which he could utilize in another area of his life. I questioned him on what he had to do every day to continue on his goal of being a non-smoker. I sought any information he had about sticking to a new plan to change oneself. By the time the session was over, we had dedicated almost thirty minutes to uncovering his ability to quit smoking and to stay smoke free for the past couple of years.

When I saw Sam two weeks later, he appeared to have made some small changes in his life. He had started looking at various social groups in his area that might be interesting to him. He also had decided to focus on a new job he found, even though he didn't like it very much. He decided to make the most of the job he had in order to work toward a better job in the future. Sam commented to me that he was using his will power to change some things for himself.

The behavioral resources our clients have are sometimes discovered by accident or by a willingness to go "off script" in our therapeutic interactions. I once worked with a ten year old boy named Barry who had been taken away from his drug addicted parents by the authorities. Custody of Barry had been given to his grandmother who lived several hours away from his home. Barry, who was very shy, had to now attend a new school. He was also very upset because he had been taken away from his parents. He began to act out at his grandmother's house because of all the life changes he had experienced. His grandmother thought it be best if he were to go to therapy and work through his issues.

Barry was smart, likeable, and shy. He talked very little to me initially. The conversation centered on why he was there to see me and what he thought of the new town where he lived in. Somehow in the course of our interaction, I made a joke in which I took on a silly accent. Barry liked that I could change my voice a little. I asked Barry if he could do different voices. He replied that he would like to do funny voices, but he didn't know how. Once I heard that, I realized that Barry could have a potential resource if he could "perform" a new behavior. Being able to make people laugh at school might allow him to make friends more easily and be more accepted.

For the rest of the session, Barry and I worked on a variety of different accents. We tried everything from Russian to Scottish accents. Some of the accents Barry could do fairly well, so we spent the remainder of our session honing in on which accent he did best and could perform the next day at school. He decided that a Scottish accent was the one he liked the best. We conducted the remainder of our session only in Scottish accents (poorly done on my part), and laughed at each other's new resource.

The next time I saw Barry, he described what had happened at school when he unleashed his new accent on his unsuspecting classmates. He stated that they all laughed and asked him to say certain things in the accent. He had received so much attention that the teacher had to ask Barry to cease and desist his Scottish interjections in class. He beamed as he told me the story. We spent the rest of the session "perfecting" his accent and playing with other voices. I spoke with his grandmother at the end of our time together, and she stated that she had noticed that Barry was a little more relaxed and had even had a phone call or two from some friends at school. Barry's conscious change in his behavior gave him access to the resource of humor which continued to serve him well as he navigated the difficult path of living in a new home and being the new kid at school.

Even behaviors that are labeled as dysfunctional can sometime be used to create new responses and resources for clients. The patterns we exhibit often feel to us as if they happen automatically or they are set in stone. If these patterns are so unconsciously ingrained, it can often be daunting to persuade the person to change, particularly if we are only using conscious mind oriented talking as our mode of therapy. Often clients are trying their best to solve their own problems, but the behaviors involved in the attempted solution only appear to make the problem worse. According to Fisch, Weakland, and Segal (1982), "something in people's attempted "solutions", the very ways they are trying to alter a problem, contributes most to the problem's maintenance or exacerbation" (p.13). Clients may be very motivated to find their own solutions, but get stuck in a loop of trying to fix the problem. The behavior they use to fix the problem merely continues to solidify the problem which, not only fails to eradicate what distresses them, but instead pulls clients down into a negative spiral of hopelessness and helplessness.

One of the first things we need to observe when clients discuss their problem is, what are the patterns emerging? We need to identify the behaviors that both create and maintain the problem. This is not seeking in depth etiology, but rather discerning what actions are maintaining the problem. In becoming aware of the behavioral patterns being exhibited, we can suggest changes in those patterns to adjust the outcome of the problem. As Fisch, et al, (1982) state, "If problem formation and maintenance are seen as parts of a vicious-circle process, in which well-intended "solution" behaviors maintain the problem, the alteration of these behaviors should interrupt the cycle and initiate resolution of the problem" (p.18). Much like the Zen Master who directs his students seeking enlightenment to perform odd activities in order to shock them out of their habitual way of responding to the world, so is the therapist directing clients to alter their behavioral patterns so that fresh new ways of responding to the problem brought to therapy can be accessed. By creating interactions so different from the clients' habitual way of behaving, it can shake up their ability to go back to the same problem in the same way. As Whitaker and Bumberry

(1988) state, "If you talk about something that's so crazy that they can't fit it into their programmed thinking process, then you leave them with a picture that's yours, not theirs, and they can begin to attach symbolism to it. They can begin to attach power to it, until it becomes a very loaded part of their life" (p.22).

By observing clients' present behavior and then making small adjustments to the behavior, we open up clients to new resources of how to respond in more effective and empowering ways. To make this happen, we, as therapists, need to find creative ways to get the client to adjust these patterns without resistance. As Rossi (2001) states, "The creative moment occurs when a habitual pattern of association is interrupted" (p.156). The moment our clients adjust their way of "doing" their problem, their brains begin associating new resources to old patterns. Just by asking a client to intentionally perform a problem pattern can create a new way of associating to the pattern. This gives more possibilities for the creation of new empowering behaviors as "there is always the possibility that if the problem maintaining cycle can be interrupted, and a more appropriate response to the problem behavior initiated, then a positive or "virtuous" cycle may begin" (Fisch, et al, 1982, p.288).

In creating a situation in which clients will experience their problem in a new way and in which they begin to question their own perceptions about the problem, we open up clients to new possibilities and resources. Because the usual order in which they have experienced their problem has changed, clients have little choice but to begin a new way of interaction with the problem. This experience will create much needed behavioral flexibility for clients, and this new found flexibility can be used as a resource to transcend the problem. As Keeney (1983) states, "In general, any problematic system requires thee ingredients for correction. First, a sufficient range of sensors to detect differences. Second, a sufficient range of varied behavior to facilitate the creation of a difference. And finally, and most importantly, the system must be able to recursively link sensors and effectors so as to provide self-correction. The therapist's job is to enter a system and participate in a way that connects their sensors and effectors as recursive parts of self-corrective feedback" (p.172).

One does not have to design long, complex, or elaborate plans in order to adjust the patterns of interaction. In many cases, adjustments to patterns can be minor and still have an impact on how patterns are experienced by clients. As Fisch, et al, (1982) state, "A small alteration is easily accepted because it seems a minor change and is also easily incorporated in daily routines." (p.117). By adjusting client patterns, even at a small level, they will have a new experience and, as previously discussed, it is in the experience where the emotional brain can change more easily. Getting our clients to do something different can have lasting effects on the problems that they previously considered as only mental. As Haley and Haley (2003) state, "Conversation does not change people unless there is a directive implicit in it" (p.182).

A couple came to therapy due to a recent domestic violence issue. The husband, Aaron, had pushed his wife, Melissa, and had physically thrown her out of the house after a full ten minutes of their screaming at each other. The neighbors called the police who intervened and arrested Aaron for domestic violence. The couple had come to therapy at the urging of their attorney, who was doing his best to make sure they could avoid further legal troubles. The couple appeared to be friendly, warm and affectionate toward each other.

When asked what had happened both of them responded

93

and detailed how Melissa, who stated she had mild Asperger's, often snaps and yells at their two children when the children misbehave. Aaron, who grew up in an abusive home where yelling often led to violence, would try to immediately calm her down. This in turn created an argument between the two of them which lasted until Aaron lost control and acted out against his wife. Aaron felt his wife's emotional outbursts were unnecessary and were harming the children's self-esteem. He saw himself in the role of the protector of the children and, as much as he loved his wife, he believed she was the villain in the situation since she could not seem to control her emotions.

Melissa admitted that she had an issue with becoming upset easily, but she thought it was due to her Asperger's since she felt out of control when the order of things in the home was changed. The couple said the children both had been diagnosed with Autism, and their behavior could often be erratic. Melissa felt helpless to control her emotional outbursts, but did want to try to change. With the court date for his domestic violence charge looming, Aaron was motivated to do what was necessary so that the court might look more favorable on a man who was actively working in therapy. He believed his wife was the reason he lost his temper since he was only trying to keep everything in the home safe and calm. Any expression of anger harkened back to the days of his youth when he would be physically abused by an angry parent.

The therapy session explored the reasons the couple sought therapy, and each party had discussed its side of the situation. It was decided that the "problem" was not a "domestic violence" issue but rather an uneven distribution of emotions in the household. I suggested to Aaron he was not helping his wife by withholding his emotions. Aaron was shocked to hear that; first, he

94

bore some responsibility for the turn of events, and second, that there needed to be more emotions in the home. I told Aaron that since he did not contribute enough emotion in the home, his wife had to pick up the slack. She had to be angry for both of them since he was unwilling to be emotional. Melissa had to become snappy and angry because there was not an equal expression of anger in the home. If Aaron wanted things to get better, he would have to insure that his wife was able to take a vacation from emoting. In order to allow her to take a break from being the emotional focal point in the home, he was to begin snapping at the kids and showing some anger.

Aaron was given the task of being the angry person in the house for one week. He was to yell at the kids instead of his wife. If his wife became anxious about what the kids were doing, she was not to yell but she was to immediately tell her husband to be angry and yell at the kids. Aaron reacted in horror after hearing this assignment while Melissa was grinning ear to ear. He felt that his yelling at the kids would irreversibly damage them. I assured him that he knew the difference between yelling at the children to reinforce boundaries and yelling at the children to needlessly degrade them. He told me he was unwilling to do this because it was against his Christian beliefs. I assured him that it is the intent of the action that is most important since the intent determines whether an action is a good behavior or a bad behavior. I also remarked that I sincerely doubted that Jesus had passively and quietly asked the money changers in the temple to leave. Aaron finally agreed to give his wife a break from emotion for a week while he assumed the role of the emotional person in the house.

When the couple came back to see me in two weeks, there was a noticeable change in their interaction. They both seemed more calm and affectionate toward each other. Melissa said that she had enjoyed her week respite from having to be the emotional one in the house. After the week concluded, she noticed that she did not seem as emotional as she was had been before the assignment of her husband to be the emotional one in the household. She found that she was more in control of herself when she snapped at the children. She had even begun to walk away and have a cooling off period before she addressed the actions of the children or her husband that bothered her.

Aaron did not enjoy his assignment at all since it was very out of character for him. He told me that the children did not know what to think about his change to an emotional father. He was glad once his week of emotion was over. At the same time he did relate that he was not getting as upset at his wife when she was angry. He seemed to be calmer about emotion in general, and he did not go into an automatic fight or flight state when someone in the home became upset. He also related that after the week of being the emotional one, he and the children seemed to bond more. He also noticed that the children and their mother laughed and played together more often.

By having Melissa halt her emotional outburst for a moment so she could let Aaron know it was time to yell at the children, Melissa found a new pattern of not immediately reacting to her emotional state. Having Aaron become the emotional person for a week forced him to experience the actions which he most feared, and to see that he had flexibility in his response to different situations. It also showed him that his wife could be something other than just a reactive presence in the house.

ENVIRONMENT

The space we inhabit can affect how we feel. Sometimes going away for a little while gives people a perspective that they may not have while in the same environment as their problem. Suggesting clients go to places where they feel more calm or empowered can assist the therapy process as this change in location may give clients access to resources. Sending clients to such diverse places as forests, jazz clubs, or shopping malls can aid them in gaining a different perspective on their issues.

Changing the location where a problem occurs can be a major step toward changing the problem. Milton Erickson once worked with a man who was chronically depressed and stayed at home all day stuck in his depression. Erickson directed the man to go to the local library and spend the whole day reading. Erickson told him that, since he was going to be depressed anyway, he might as well be depressed outside his home. The man followed the directive and spent a few days at the library. He ended up interacting with other people and even found a new friend who shared one of his interests. The man eventually began interacting with people more often, and his depression rapidly decreased. Erickson's directive of simply changing his environment was a strategic move to get the man out of his social isolation, which made his depression worse, and to create new connections and experiences.

I worked with a couple who were locked in a pattern of frustration and anger in their interactions. After a couple of sessions, with little change in their behavior, I asked them what they missed the most about the early days of their relationship. Both made comments about how they each felt free to be open with each other. They thought this openness was due to their being so young and also having a childlike sense of wonder about each other. I asked if they were interested in taking a break from their dysfunctional pattern to allow themselves to feel that childlike sense of wonder again, if only for a day. I asked if they were willing to go to Disneyland to rediscover the childlike wonder which brought them together. Both were surprised and said they had not been to Disneyland since they were both very young. They agreed to take an upcoming weekend, put their arguments on hold, and travel to Disneyland. When they returned, they appeared more open and willing to do the necessary work to heal their relationship. They had only argued once as they were leaving to go on the trip. Something about being at Disneyland unconsciously reminded them that they had access to the resources of fun and wonder within their relationship.

Change in our environment does not require a trip somewhere. Sometimes rearranging the furniture or painting the walls in one's own living space can aid in shifting how we deal with our problem. If clients believe that they have no control in their lives, I may ask them to change something in their home. This action may remind them that they do have some control to change something about their lives. I once had a client who dealt with some of her frustrations by purchasing a book on "feng shui", a Chinese philosophical system that works to harmonize people with the environment by changing the placement of items within the environment. She noticed more calm and peace within herself after she adjusted her furniture in her home to the specifications of the feng shui plan. I cannot state with any authority that the feng shui was responsible for her change of mood; however, her adjustment of her home environment may have caused her to feel more in control of some aspect of her life whereas previously she had felt directionless.

My own hardship of being alone after a painful divorce was helped by changing my outdoor environment. I dug up several old plants in my backyard and planted new ones. I put out fresh mulch and rearranged the potted bushes near my patio. I also bought a new ornament to sit among the plants, a sculpture which for me, symbolized the balancing of both good and bad in life. I found that this one change in my environment gave me a sense of hope and a feeling of energy. Unconsciously it reminded me that we can always change things and start over in surprising ways.

SPIRITUALITY

The idea that some aspects of the psychotherapy process can be spiritual is certainly not new. Throughout our history the area of healing, both physical and psychological, was the domain of men and women identified as shamans, priests/ priestesses, and medicine people. Some psychotherapy theorists believe there is little difference between the therapy process and spirituality. Corbett (2011) suggests "there is no need to speak of psychotherapy and spirituality as if they were radically different separate disciplines, because the spirit manifests itself by means of the psyche, producing soulful experience" (p.2)

Asking questions about our clients' religious or spiritual beliefs can be an important part of the therapeutic process, and, more importantly, can be a quick way to find resources that will help clients to transform their present situation. Some therapists are reluctant to ask about the spiritual aspects of their clients' lives for fears of intruding too deeply into their clients' privacy. Some are reluctant to discuss spirituality with their clients due to their own discomfort with the topic. Corbett (2011) has found that many times "the therapist may be uneasy about acknowledging a spiritual dimension to his or her work, especially if his or her professional training was limited to a materialistic or reductionist approach to the psyche" (p.5).

I have found that no matter what my clients' spiritual beliefs are, if those beliefs are positive and helpful to the client, then they should be thoroughly explored as potential resources. As Corbett (2011) states, "In its widest sense, one's spirituality may simply be one's personal way of dealing with life's ultimate questions, or whatever is of the highest value to the individual" (p.2). We, as therapists, need to be comfortable asking about the role of spirituality in our client's lives. Clients may already perform spiritual based actions which could be utilized to gain a new perspective on their problems.

Spiritually themed actions and rituals can be healing for people who have become disconnected from their own spiritual resources. Rituals can be a great comfort to clients during times of emotional and physical hardships. According to Gilligan (1993), "Ritual may be regarded as an intense, experiential-symbolic structure that recreates or transforms identity" (p.239). Rituals can help supply clients with a distraction from their present problem and also activate a sense of hope and aliveness needed in navigating the challenges of living. The renewal of such rituals and spiritual activities should be honored and encouraged in clients who previously found comfort in them.

Sometimes the problematic patterns clients are performing can be seen as a ritual, which unfortunately strengthens the very problem clients seek to overcome. As Gilligan states, "many symptoms presented by therapy clients may be expressions of dysfunctional rituals in which individuals recreate a negative self-identity characterized by self-abuse and helplessness" (p.240). If we frame our clients' problem as an ongoing ritual, then we may need to create a new special ritual to disrupt the patterns of the previous ritual. This new ritual can be seen as a way to offer new options to clients for responding to the old problem.

Spirituality can also create a sense of connection with others of similar beliefs. This sense of connection is very important for clients since it also can act as a support system for them outside of the therapy room. Much has been written about the need for clients to have a support system which increases positive therapeutic outcomes. I once worked with a client who was an atheist. He had no aspect of spirituality in his life and his connection with others was minimal at best. I suggested he might join a group of atheists who met once a month to discuss atheism. He took me up on my idea and found a group of people with similar beliefs to himself. His interactions with his atheist group led to him feeling connected to something other than his own sense of helplessness.

Other actions we can encourage in our spiritually minded clients are such things as reading sacred literature, meditation, and spiritually related journal writing. I have often told clients to find an empowering quote from spiritual literature that moves them and then write it down multiple times on a piece of paper. They are then to take the paper and display it some place in their home where they feel most at peace. When they are dealing with the inevitable trials and tribulations of life, they are directed to go to that special place and read the spiritual quotes. Most of the time clients find this action to be helpful in reminding them that they have a connection to something greater than themselves.

CHAPTER 5: THE CALLING

Edward, a sixty-year-old man, came to therapy due to his being physically assaulted several months earlier. Edward was an exterminator and while spraying for insects at an apartment complex, was attacked by a resident. The resident, who was on drugs, thought Edward was trying to break in his home to kill him. Edward now has to walk with a cane and lost one of his eyes in the assault. He remembers very little about the incident, other than turning around and seeing the man lunge at him. The police were called by another resident who watched Edward be attacked by the man with a baseball bat. The resident thought the man left the scene of the attack because he thought Edward had died. Edward was rushed to the hospital and had been recovering from the attack for the past several months. Edward had been dealing with issues of sleeplessness, anxiety, and depression due to his inability to perform many physical activities he did prior to the assault. His wife began noticing changes in Edward's mood and pushed him to find someone to talk with about his emotions.

The transcript picks up after the initial introductions and client history were discussed.

T: Therapist

C: Client (Edward)

T: At this point, how are you feeling about the situation?

C: Logically, I know it is over, but I still get anxious thinking about it. I also get pretty angry that I can't do what I used to do. I have always worked, and I don't think that will happen again.

T: Do you mean "work" as in employment or "work" in general?

C: Either.

T: How are you limited from working in general?

C: I can't get around without this cane, and my legs aren't working too good. Obviously, one of my eyes is gone which affects my ability to see things as I used to do.

T: So you are feeling like you have been put out to pasture?

C: (chuckles) Yes.

T: It has to be tough for you if you have always been a worker.

C: Yeah, I've been working in one way or another since I can remember. I grew up in Chicago and was always working a job or two. A couple of years ago my wife got a job down south, so we moved here. I had retired as an aviation mechanic, and I thought we could lower our overhead by moving. It is much cheaper to live down here.

T: It is.

C: I decided that I couldn't just sit around and not do anything, so I got a job as an exterminator. I like having a set schedule and working. The job also got me outdoors which I enjoy. Most of the time I didn't interact much with people as I would just show up at the corporate accounts and do my job and then move on to the next one. When I was done at the end of the day I felt like I had done my time and went home feeling pretty good. Since I got hurt I haven't felt that way because I have been stuck inside and unable to do much.

Here Edward has stated what resources he needs. He stated he enjoys staying busy, being outdoors, and having a schedule. Since those things have been taken from him he has less resources to deal with the trauma of his attack.

T: You have been sitting a lot?

C: Yeah, too much.

T: What kind of mobility do you presently have?

C: I can get around with this cane, but as you saw I have a limp when I walk.

T: How about upper body?

C: Other than my eye, everything above the waist is good. My shoulders ache sometimes, but that may have been due to the attack. At my age, it takes much longer to heal.

T: Do you have much pain?

C: Not intense pain at this point. I did have some a good while back, but now it is mostly aches instead of sharp pain.

T: So you can do things with your hands?

C: Yeah. I'm glad my hands weren't injured. I like to tinker with repairing things for fun, although I haven't done that in a while.

Edward gives another resource in his enjoyment of "tinkering" with things. He has not taken this action for some time, but it could possibly help his mood.

T: What do you like about tinkering with things?

C: I guess I like seeing how things fit together and feeling a sense of accomplishment that I can fix what is wrong. That is probably why I liked my job in aviation because I could get paid to tinker (laughs).

T: It is always great when you can get paid to play.

C: You bet. I liked trouble shooting and finding out what wasn't working. It was kind of like being a detective. I would look for clues as to why things weren't working like they should.

T: "Edward the Aviation Detective"? It sounds like it could be a television show.

C: (laughs) Maybe. I don't know how many people would be excited by the show though. Maybe other aviation mechanics? (laughs)

T: What does your wife think about how you are doing these days?

C: She is the one who pushed me to come in and talk to somebody. She could tell that I was getting a little depressed. I'm not one to talk about myself much so I usually keep those things private. I did realize that I wasn't feeling better after a while, so I decided to seek somebody out to talk about what happened.

T: Sometimes it is good to talk to someone we don't know to get a different perspective.

C: Sure. I just don't feel like I have much to offer anyone these days. I just can't do what I used to do.

T: You mentioned you liked to tinker with things. When did you first get into doing that?

C: I have always enjoyed taking things apart and putting them back together. Even when I was a child, I would take my toys apart and put them back together. Most of the time the toys would still work. Sometimes they wouldn't (laughs). When I was a teenager, I took shop in high school and loved it. I also got into working on cars when I was a teenager.

T: Did you do that in high school?

C: No. I had an uncle who worked at a mechanic shop and he would let me come by in the evenings and work on the cars with him. Sometimes we would sit and talk with the other guy who worked there and just talk about cars. I have always loved cars. I really like working on them. I learned about fixing engines and even body work from my uncle. What he taught me helped when I moved into learning to be an aviation mechanic.

T: When was the last time you worked on a car?

C: (laughs) It has been a while.

T: How long?

C: Oh, I don't know. Maybe nine months or so.

T: Do you miss it?

C: Yeah, I miss being able to do a lot of things.

T: Have you tried to work on a car at all recently?

C: No.

T: I was thinking that maybe since you were not able to work outside the home, maybe you could spend some of your free time working on a car?

C: I don't know. It is hard for me to get around.

T: I get that. I also noticed you are able to walk with that cane pretty well.

C: I try to get around and not ask for any help.

T: Yes, so I am thinking that you could possibly be able to go outside and tinker with a car. Do you have any cars you could tinker with at your home?

C: I do. I have two cars that I would like to fix up. I just haven't done much since I got hurt.

T: I understand. I was just thinking that maybe you could go out, even for a few minutes a day, and play on a car. This might help occupy some of your time.

C: Yeah, I get bored a lot. I am so used to working all the time. I have been pretty upset that I can't get around like I used to before I got hurt.

T: I am wondering if you could do a few minor things on one of your cars, even with how you are feeling now?

C: I guess I could do some small stuff. I am ok working underneath the car and I have jacks that I can use to be able to get to where I need to work.

T: Oh, wow. You are really set up then. You are serious about this car stuff, huh?

C: (laughs) Yeah, I used to really enjoy working on them. I had a couple that I fixed up and then sold.

T: So you were able to make some money on them?

C: Yeah, I would go get a car that needed a good bit of work and then I would fix it up enough to where it was running and then I would sell it. I didn't make much. To be honest, as long as I made what I spent on buying it and the parts, I would have been happy.

T: You love it that much?

C: I do. Working on cars was kind of like a time where I could relax and get away from everything.

Here is another potential resource for Edward being able to manage his emotional state. His working on cars gave him a feeling of relaxation.

T: I envy people who have something that really inspires them.

C: I don't know if I am inspired or not, but I get excited when I get to work on a car. I really like the classic cars a lot.

T: Do you ever go to car shows?

C: Not too often. I get more enjoyment out of finding an old beat up car and making it run again.

T: That is really cool that you have that kind of gift.

C: (laughs) Yeah, I feel like I have always had this calling to work with my hands.

T: A calling? Do you mean like you were destined to work with your hands?

C: Yeah. I feel like I was put here to do that. Now I feel like I can't seem to do what I used to do.

T: So you are telling me that you feel like you are not following your calling because what happened to you?

C: It feels that way.

T: If you were to work for just a little bit every day on one of those cars, would that help you feel like you were following your calling?

C: I don't know. I feel like I should be doing more, but with my body all banged up…

T: (interrupts) But, wait a minute! You told me that you were destined to work with your hands and you can get around a little bit with the cane. You also told me you could use the jacks.

C: Yeah.

T: If that is the case, then you can do a few things, right?

C: I guess so.

T: If you were able to fix up one of those cars enough for someone to drive, how would you feel about that?

C: It would be great.

T: How quickly could you get one of those cars going?

C: I guess I could get one of them going in a couple of weeks. I just need to put in a new alternator, battery, and some belts. It won't look pretty….

T: That doesn't matter at this point. Would it then be a car that someone could ride to and from work in?

C: Yeah.

T: So by fixing it up and selling it to someone, you could be helping them get a low cost vehicle to be able to get to work in?

C: I guess so.

T: Edward, maybe that is part of your calling?

C: What is?

T: You tinkering with these cars and giving people a low cost way to get to get a car. There are so many people who need transportation and just don't have the money to buy a nice car. At this stage they need something that runs, no matter what it looks like. This may sound strange to hear and I could totally be wrong, but I am just wondering if maybe you had to slow down in order for you to fulfill the obligation to your calling.

C: I don't understand what you mean.

T: What I mean is that now that you are not able to work a "regular" job, you are now in a perfect position to begin focusing more on your calling.

C: Are you saying I was supposed to get attacked?

T: No, not at all. I am merely wondering if for some reason you have been now presented with an opportunity to follow more of your calling than you have in recent times. You were working your job as an exterminator to stay busy, not as a calling. It sounded like you were doing more of your calling when you worked in aviation. I am just thinking that maybe this time is now open for you to truly and completely to follow your calling.

C: You know, the preacher at my church talked about being called the other day. He said it happens in times when you least expect it.

T: Hmmm, that's interesting.

C: I don't know. It doesn't feel like I am being called.

T: What would that feel like?

C: I guess I don't know.

T: If you fixed up one of those cars, would it help someone?

C: It could. I could sell it really cheap.

T: By doing that it sounds like you are performing an act of service to your fellow man.

C: I guess so. You know, it is funny. I talked to someone the other day who told me that transportation was one of the main reasons people who live out in the country can't seem to get ahead. They don't have a car to get into the city to work and there are no buses that go out there.

T: If someone had a cheap car, then it could help him or her to put food on the table.

C: Yeah.

T: And if someone had a calling to help others through using his hands, then he might do a lot of good for others while having fun himself.

At this point Edward becomes quiet and is contemplating what has been said.

C: (laughs) You're making me think, Doc.

T: That's my job.

C: I guess so.

T: I'm not telling you what to do, I'm just suggesting you consider what is unfolding in front of you.

C: I don't know…it will be hard for me to get out there.

T: When you say "hard", how do you mean…

C: I mean it will be physically hard.

T: I'm sure it will be in the beginning. Do you think you won't be able to do it?

C: Nah, I can do it. I just think it will be really hard.

T: The nice thing about not having to work a regular schedule is that you are able to do as much or as little as you feel like.

C: Sure.

T: When do you think you could get started on the car?

C: I don't know, maybe next week?

T: Ok. What day next week?

C: Hmm….Monday?

T: Ok. What time Monday?

C: Probably in the morning, maybe around nine o'clock.

T: That sounds great. What will it be like to be back working on something you love?

C: I guess it will be good. I have been getting so tired of just sitting around.

T: I get it. So Monday at nine o'clock you will be taking your time working on one of those cars to get it running. That car could potentially help someone else be able to get to work and make a living, right?

C: I guess so.

T: Will you call my office later in the day Monday and leave a message for me as to how it went working on the car?

C: Sure.

T: I am very curious how you will be feeling after you get back in the swing of things.

C: Ok.

Edward forgot to call the office on Monday, but returned to therapy in three weeks. He stated he had begun working on one of his cars. He stated that it was not easy, but it gave him a feeling of satisfaction to know he could do it. He also stated that he had talked with his pastor about repairing cars. Edward and his pastor came up with an idea to start a church program where old cars could be bought, repaired, and then given to families who desperately needed transportation. Edward was visibly excited when talking about the potential to start this program. He volunteered to do the work for free as long as his expenses for parts were covered. Edward's mood was lighter, and he reported that he had less rumination on the events which originally brought him to therapy. He also reported that he was able to relax in the evenings and sleep better. Over the next few sessions Edward found that he could do more things than he thought he could and began considering it a challenge to figure out how to work around his physical limitations when working on cars.

CHAPTER 6: NAME THAT FRAME: THE IMPORTANCE OF REFRAMING

One of the most important things therapists can do in a therapy session is be of aware of the context in which clients present information. The context in which we perceive and receive information can often determine our mental, behavioral, and emotional responses. Contexts of inflexibility and disempowerment create inflexible and disempowering responses. Contexts of possibility and strength create possibility laden and strengths based responses. By being aware of the context that is being presented in a therapy session, therapists can enact shifts in clients' perspectives more easily and more efficiently.

How we experience the world around us is based on how we place our experiences into certain categories. Those categories are created solely by us and often have a different meaning and value for us than the reality of the experience itself. One experience can be placed into the "good" category and another placed into the "bad" category. The categorical labeling of these experiences can differ widely between people. For example, one person may label a divorce as "a tragedy" and another person may label the same experience as "a gift from the gods". I remember a colleague telling a client that some people say "Oh my God!" when a relationship is over, while others say "Thank God!" The ending of a relationship is the event, but it is in the context of how we frame that event that creates our responses. "Context determines the value of any pattern, not the pattern itself. Any pattern has the potential to be helpful or harmful, depending on the context in which it is applied." (Yapko, 2001, p.34)

Once we have had an experience and we then place it into a

specific category, it is often very difficult to view the experience as belonging to another category. We begin to think of the category as objective reality, rather than a subjective perception based on the category where we placed it. If we then hear someone else view the experience in a different category, we often feel that the person who sees the experience differently is somehow out of touch with reality. We "know" that our experience is in a specific category so there can be no other category for it. If, however, we are open to the possibility that the experience may fit into another category, then it is difficult for us to see the experience in the old way. As Whitaker and Bumberry (1988) state, "We all filter our experiences of living through a relatively narrow number of constructs. It's the richness or poverty of these constructs that goes a long way in determining the subjective experience of being." (p.75)

The category in which we place experiences is called a "frame of experience". If we want our clients to shift their perception of their experience, then we need to "reframe" the experience. This means we will need to create a new category in which to place their experience. This is why attempting "solutions" for problems often do not lead to generative change. If the frame of experience is still firmly rooted in the frame of the problem, then the "solution" has to take place solely inside the problem frame. It is when clients' experience is shifted out of the problem frame that real healing begins. If the problem remains a problem, then the client and the therapist will continue to react to the problem and continue to be stuck inside the limiting frame. According to Furman and Ahola (1994), "It has become evident that one's attempted solution is always contingent upon how one defines and explains the problem. A change in the way one thinks about a problem can bring about a drastic change in the way one attempts to solve it." (p.64)

A problem maintains itself due to the context it occurs in. If a therapist can change the meaning that is perceived by the client, a shift in the context will take place. How a problem is understood and experienced is often determined by the client's point of view about the situation. The original cause of the problem may have little to do with the continuation of the problem. The problem continues because the client sees it as a problem. The client is now stuck within a context that identifies the problem. This is one of the reasons that strange interventions, which can appear to have little to do with the problem can work in deconstructing the problem. The intervention is not directly tied to the problem, but rather the context in which it appears. To quote Keeney (1983), "A lens, or frame of reference determines the pattern we see, whether it is up or down, distorted or not. A change of lens always invokes a period of initial confusion or transition. If an observer can endure the crisis of transition, a new frame will result in an alternative order." (p.155)

When interventions are directed toward a wider perspective, it can have far reaching consequences for clients. If clients have had a profound shift in how they perceive a situation, then the possibilities for clients exhibiting new behaviors are much more probable. If clients' perceptions of an event no longer create reactive behaviors, then the change in perception has created a new resource. As Nardone (1996) states, "The change and solution of personal and interpersonal human problems can, therefore, only be reached by way of a change in the perceptive and reactive modalities which the patient experiences reality" (p.82). It is not strictly a specific situation which is maintaining a problem, but rather "problem persistence derives from a patient's perceptions and perspective on the reality that forces him or her to have the so-called dysfunctional behavioral reactions toward this reality." (Nardone, 1996, p.87)

Our experience of life becomes limited and painful when we do not understand that it is we who create our own frames of experience. When we act within those frames of reference and try to change the experience within the frame, we flounder because the material inside the frame cannot change. Only the frame of reference can change. Since one's frame of reference determines the patterns that are demonstrated, it is in comparing different frames where therapists begin to offer opportunities for change to clients. Even though the details of clients' stories have not changed, their perceptions about the details have changed. What previously may have been difficult for them to live with, may now be livable within a new frame. A new frame creates a new meaning which may alleviate long term suffering. As Frankl (2006) notes, "Suffering ceases to be suffering at the moment it finds a meaning." (p.135).

When we are dealing with life's challenges, we often have very little access to positive resources because those resources are outside of our frame of reference. As Gilligan (1986) states, "The assumption is that in a problem state the self experiences little connection to essential resources. The resources may either be outside (i.e. functionally dissociated from) the problem frame (e.g. the person may lose his/her ability to ask for what he/she wants) or operating in a rigid self-dissociated manner within the frame (e.g. the person may only ask for what he/she wants in a shrill, ineffective manner). In both cases, the rigidity of the frame allows no new movement from the outside or within its boundaries" (p.169).

To effectively move beyond the limited perception of a problem, therapists must learn to reframe the problem in a way which generates new resources for the client. The generation of new resources due to a shift in the perception of the experience is often enough to create changes in multiple areas of the client's life. People unknowingly accept the context in which they live their lives. When the context a person is using to direct his or her life is changed, this will often lead to an adjustment in the person's habitual perception and action. According to Watzlawick, Weakland and Fisch (1974): "To reframe, then means to change the conceptual and/or emotional setting or viewpoint in relation to which a situation is experienced and to place it in another frame which fits the 'facts' of the same concrete situation equally well or even better, and thereby changes its entire meaning" (p.95) To be successful at reframing means that the therapist "must lift the problem out of the symptom frame and into another frame that does not carry the implication of unchangeability." (Watzlawick, et al, 1974, p.102).

Finding solutions are not bad per se, but why not find solutions within a more resourceful frame? For example, imagine you have a client who is grieving the end of a long term relationship. In passing, she states that not being in the relationship might allow her to have time and money to open the business she always wanted to open. At this point, why not apply the solution focused perspective to the resource of starting a business? Shifting her away from the relationship pain and toward the dream of entrepreneurship could create amazing resources for her. Focusing on what she will need to do, what fears she may have about starting a business, and where she could get information on funding, will do more to create resources within the client than excessively talking about the ending of the relationship. If she has fears about opening her dream business, then apply some cognitive therapy to her fears about the business instead of more discussion of her relationship. Most tools used in psychotherapy work better in the frame of a resource rather than in a frame of a problem. Once the frame has been changed, clients are usually more open to following treatment plans. As Musikantow (2015) states, "resistance occurs less frequently, because the directives that the therapist offers make sense within that context. They are congruent and logical given the experiential reality created by the frame." (p.1740)

A couple once came to me for help in managing their arguments about how they spent money. The wife had children from a previous marriage, and she and her new husband were the primary caregivers for the children. The children saw their biological father once a month. When the children visited their father they were showered with gifts. They received whatever they wanted and enjoyed their time with him very much. This caused animosity in the couple because they were working hard simply to take care of all the expenses related to rearing the children, while the father was free to spend money on "fun things". Due to working hard to try and make ends meet, while knowing they could not give their children the "fun" things, the couple often bickered about how much of their money was spent or saved. The frame of the problem they brought to therapy was of impoverished financial resources. They were both upset that they could not afford the fun things their children wanted and angry at the children's father for being so carefree with his gifts, while withholding financial help for important things, such as school clothes and medical bills.

I asked if the children's father was emotionally mature enough to handle the responsibilities for the children. They both answered very firmly that the father was very immature and only was able to interact with the children as a friend and not as a parent. They said that he did not give the children enough boundaries when they visit and was more focused on having fun with them. As I considered what they said, it occurred to me that there was a balance in this interaction between the couple, the children, and the children's father. I wondered out loud if the children's father was showing love the only way he knew how. I conjectured that maybe since unconsciously he knew he could never provide the love, structure, and boundaries that are important for children, he overcompensated in the only way he knew how, which was to spend money on fun things. I also opined that it is such a good lesson for the children to know that, even though the couple was not able to give them elaborate gifts, the most important parenting duties were being provided by the couple. I told them that the children were so fortunate to have the presence of good, mature parents, while also getting to enjoy the latest toys and games provided by their father. I told the couple how lucky their children were to have the best of both worlds.

The couple had never thought of the situation in those terms. We discussed what a relief it would be to not worry so much about providing the fun stuff since the children's father was already doing that. Since their children were not doing without, quite the contrary, rather having the best of both worlds, the couple could begin saving more money and focusing on being the best mature, stable parents they could be. They also began to see how the children's father's behavior, previously irritating and frustrating, was actually a blessing since it relieved them of having to buy all the latest gadgets for the children. The frame of the session had changed from "impoverished financial resources" into "the best of both worlds". Nothing had changed in the scenario brought to therapy except the perception of the couple. This moved them toward their innate resources, that of mature parents. Much of their disappointment and anger toward the children's father, and each other, disappeared.

A Simple and Easy to Reframe

1. Become aware of what interpretation of the problem the client is currently perceiving.

This requires that therapists do not get too stuck on the small details of the problem. Therapists need to be able to see the big picture and the theme. Sometimes I will ask clients to give me the problem in one sentence so that I can be clear on their perceptions and not too distracted by extraneous details. By knowing clearly and specifically what clients perceive as a problem, we can more easily open up other possibilities for perceiving the situation.

2. Examine what other possible interpretations of the problem could exist.

At this point, we begin by asking clients if the problem is a problem due to such things as the setting it takes place in, the people who are involved in it, or other patterns of interaction. For example, if a client has issues with a spouse who does not express emotions, the therapist could suggest the spouse's lack of emotions protects the family from unnecessary anger.

3. When the most interesting alternative interpretation comes to your mind, immediately share it with the client.

Sometimes a reframe can sound strange, funny, deeply profound, or really weird. It is not our reaction to the reframe that matters, but rather how clients react to the new information.

4. Observe how this new information affects the client. If the outcome is a shift in his or her perspective, build upon it. If no shift occurs, then get rid of the reframe and move on.

What really matters in designing a reframe is whether or not the reframe resonates with clients because a new way of viewing an old problem, can create a change in the problem.

Judy came to therapy because she was afraid to drive her car. She was able to drive where she wanted to go, but she spent the entire trip frightened and panicked. Her fear was due to a car accident she had a year previously. Judy was tired of being frightened whenever she got into an automobile. She felt helpless and was frustrated that she just "couldn't get over it".

I asked Judy what her greatest fear about driving was for her. She quickly replied, "Death". She proceeded to tell me about her car accident. A truck pulled in too close in front of her, and she swerved to miss it. Her swerving caused her car to go off the interstate and roll over several times finally landing against a tree. She had only minor injuries, which had surprised the paramedics who had been called to the scene. Judy said that even the highway patrol officers were amazed that she had survived the accident.

I told her that I understood and that it was natural for anyone who had been through such an ordeal to feel frightened that it could happen again. I then asked her why she believed she had not been seriously injured in the accident. Judy smiled and said,

"God was watching out for me. He had to be, or I would not be here talking with you today." I could clearly see a resource when she uttered those words.

"So you think God was watching out for you and was protecting you?" I asked. "Absolutely. Without a shadow of a doubt." Judy answered. "So you think God saved you from this wreck and continues to keep watch over you?" I asked. "Yes sir, he does!" Judy said with a large smile. I thought for a moment and then told Judy that, if God was protecting her during the most amazing accident, it was obvious that she had something special to do here on earth. I then wondered that if she is here to do something special, then it would be highly unlikely that she would die in a car wreck anytime soon. Judy thought for a moment and then agreed with me. I continued to elaborate on this theme by wondering if it was possible that the car wreck could have been God's way of showing her that she would be alright in the future. If she could survive such an extreme event, then she had proof that she would be safe in the future. The old frame of reference which had surrounded her accident, and driving in general, was "potential death". The new frame was that God was watching over her, and she had special work to do on earth.

After our session Judy felt more in control of her anxiety while driving. She admitted to sometimes getting a little nervous when there was heavy traffic, but she always reminded herself that God was watching over her and God would not take her until her work on earth was done. By utilizing her faith as a resource and adjusting her perception of her accident, the frame surrounding the accident shifted and allowed her to feel more comfortable driving.

Examples of reframing problematic behavior

Anger – the courage to show one's fear

124

Fear – being able to recognize danger quickly

Impulsive – not fearful of being open to the spontaneous

Controlling – focused on ensuring structure in the ever changing world

Argumentative – courageous enough to stick to one's opinion

Reframing is one of the most essential skills a therapist can have. There are times where little in a situation can be changed other than how the client frames the situation. Reframing helps our clients to create a new reality around their problem. By opening up possibilities and different ways they may experience their situation, it offers them a choice on how they can respond to that situation.

CHAPTER 7: THE PORCELAIN DOLL

Anna came to therapy a day after being discharged from the hospital. She was sent to the hospital by her psychiatrist due to her suicidal ideation. She had been dealing with an addiction to prescription drugs after several painful surgeries. Anna felt better after being stabilized in the hospital, but was still wrestling with depression. She was struggling with insomnia and worried about taking medication due to her addiction issues. For the past two years she had been mostly staying in bed or watching television because of her recovery from her surgeries and the effects of the medication to which she had become addicted.

T: Therapist

C: Client (Anna)

T: So you just got out of the hospital?

C: Yeah, yesterday.

T: I am glad you were able to come out of the hospital so quickly.

C: Me too. I didn't like it in there, but my doctor thought I needed to go because of comments I made.

T: What kind of comments?

C: I told her that I didn't want to live anymore and I couldn't see a future for myself. I guess she thought I was going to kill myself. I was pretty low. I feel better today. I still don't feel that great, but I am better today.

T: I'm glad to hear it.

C: I have been struggling with being addicted to the pain medication I have had to take.

T: Why did you start taking pain medicine?

C: I had surgery two years ago, and it didn't go well. They had to operate twice and my recovery time was much longer than expected. I had to take pain medicine to be able to function but I eventually got addicted to it. You know, I couldn't live without it. At least that was what it felt like.

T: Yeah.

C: I was able to get off the medicine, but I then went into a deep depression which ended up with me in the hospital. I can't sleep at night and my doctor is worried about the medicine I am on for sleep.

T: I can understand that.

C: Yeah. I just can't seem to sleep. I get an hour or so, and I wake up. I am tired a lot because of it. The medicine does help me calm down at night.

T: Do you feel anxious at night?

C: Yes, if I don't have my sleep medicine I am really anxious at night. I wake up anxious and I stay that way all day. I can't seem to calm down.

T: What do you usually do to cope with your anxiety?

C: I haven't done much. In the past the medicine I was addicted to helped me, but I'm not using it now. I thought about getting some exercise. Maybe that could help.

T: Sure. What kind of exercise?

C: I could start walking for twenty minutes a day when the kids are at school.

T: That would be great. How many kids do you have?

C: I have two girls.

T: How old?

C: Ten and eight.

T: Are you close to them?

C: I want to be but these past two years have been hard. They only know me as the mom who is in the bed and stays on the couch.

T: Yeah, they will be surprised when they seeing you do something different.

C: For sure.

T: They may even wonder what is wrong with mom. She keeps getting up and doing things. This isn't normal!

C: (laughs) Yeah.

T: I feel like you have been stuck for a while.

C: Yes. I feel like I have lost a lot of my life. I want to change things, but people keep expecting me to be the way I have been in the past.

T: Which people?

C: My parents and my doctor.

T: Oh.

C: I understand that they have had a lot of time to see me do things which weren't good in the past, but it hurts my feelings when they just assume that I will keep doing the same things.

T: So they will really be surprised when they see you becoming more active and feeling better?

C: Yes.

T: Good. Are you presently married?

C: Yes, my husband has been so supportive through all of this. He just wants his wife back. I haven't been his wife for two years because of how I felt and the medicine made me change a lot.

T: So he will not only be surprised to see the new you, but also to get his wife back?

C: Yeah, he has been through it all with me. He supports me the best he can. It has been really tough.

T: It sounds like it.

C: I just stay so anxious so much. It is like I can't settle down.

T: Have you always felt this anxious?

C: No. It really is only the last couple of years.

T: You must have a lot of nervous energy that needs to come out.

C: Maybe.

T: No, seriously. I wonder if the past two years has been such a block to your creativity that the energy inside had nowhere to go. It was stuck in you with no outlet. You said yourself that you felt stuck.

C: Yes.

T: If energy has nowhere to go it just kind of builds up and rolls around inside us. We feel like we can't sit still. The energy needs to go somewhere. This is why I like to hear that you are thinking about going walking. This will help a little of that energy to leave.

C: Good.

T: What have you done that is creative in the last year?

C: Nothing.

T: Nothing?

C: Nothing.

T: I think this may be a part of the problem.

C: How?

T: When we are not doing creative things we can feel stuck and the energy builds up. You have been so focused on unpleasant things that your creativity has nowhere to go. It builds up and you get anxious.

C: Ok.

Anna's issues with anxiety are reframed as blockages in creativity. Becoming more creative is a more inspiring goal than eradicating anxiety.

T: I think you might want to consider changing some things up in your life pretty quickly to get some of that energy out. When was the last time you redecorated your home?

C: Oh, wow. It has probably been a little over two years ago.

T: Two years ago was when you started having those surgeries, right?

C: Yes.

T: Yeah, I think the surgeries, addiction, medicine,…all those things have blocked your creativity for too long. I want you to consider redecorating some rooms in your home. Is that something you feel you could do?

C: I could probably do a little bit in the house. I don't know if my husband would be happy with me spending much money.

T: You don't have to spend much to redecorate. Sometimes just moving some furniture around helps creativity because you are using that energy.

C: Yeah, I could rearrange some things.

T: What room would you want to rearrange first?

C: My living room.

T: What would you do in there?

C: I could move a small table.

T: What about painting the room?

C: Hmmm…..I really like the paint in the room. It is a rust color. It goes really well with my curtains.

T: What about painting just one wall in the room?

C: (*She thinks for a moment*) Yeah, I could do that. That might look nice.

T: What color?

C: Maybe a tan or beige color.

T: That would make the rust walls pop out, wouldn't it?

C: Yeah.

T: And one small can of paint would be all you would need. That wouldn't cost much.

C: Yeah, so my husband wouldn't be too upset about that.

T: Certainly. You could paint that one wall tan and make it a symbol of things to come. It can represent the new change that the family is taking. Do you have any pictures in the living room now?

C: We have a painting but no pictures. I have family pictures, but I don't have them out in the living room.

T: You may want to put those pictures on the wall. Since this wall will represent your new focus in life, I'm guessing that your family is going to be getting a lot more of your attention.

C: Yes.

T: So this is why you may want to put those pictures on the wall. It lets you know where your new focus is.

C: Yes, I need to do that. I have put my family on hold for too long because of the past two years.

T: Yeah, and them seeing that one wall, that one special wall, that represents your future, lets them know that they are your future.

C: Yes. (*Anna is starting to get emotional*)

T: What a great way to get that energy out and let your family know that the real you is back.

C: Yeah. I will do it.

T: What else could you redecorate in your home?

C: I would love to change up my kitchen, but my husband wouldn't go for it.

T: Why is that?

C: I want new counter tops and cabinets and that is too much money right now.

T: Could you paint those cabinets?

C: I could, but I don't want to spend too much money.

T: Sure, I understand. You may find some nice paint on sale for the cabinets when you go get the tan paint for the living room though.

C: That true.

T: Just something to think about.

C: Yeah.

T: What will it be like for you to have that wall set up with those wonderful family pictures, knowing that you did it yourself?

C: It will be great. It will be a new beginning.

T: A new beginning for everyone.

C: Yes, for everyone.

T: How surprised will those girls of yours be when they see mom taking charge in the house by painting and moving furniture?

C: (laughs) Very surprised!

T: I want to warn you that if you start redecorating your space, they may want you to help them with their space. I am not saying it will happen, but be prepared for it if it does.

C: Yes, they usually want to do what I am doing.

T: So maybe you three could work together on doing some things?

C: Yeah, that would be nice.

T: They may want their rooms painted.

C: They probably will.

T: That is the great thing about painting a wall. It doesn't require you to have to focus too much on the action. You could do it with very little effort.

C: Yeah.

T: It is not like having to paint one of those intricate designs on a porcelain doll.

C: I used to have porcelain dolls.

T: Really?

C: Yes, I still have them, but they are packed up. I loved them. I liked to collect them.

T: What did you like the most about them?

C: I don't really know. I always thought they were pretty. A lot of work went into them. I haven't seen them in years.

T: Where are they?

C: They are packed up in large box in my closet. When I first got married I had them out in the bedroom, but my husband said they creeped him out. I put them up because they bothered him. He is so silly sometimes. I wanted to share the dolls with my daughters, but they weren't interested in them. I had not thought about those dolls in a long time.

T: Isn't it interesting that of all the things that I have said today, that something about porcelain dolls would come out of my mouth?

C: Yes.

T: I take that as a sign that you need to unpack those dolls. Maybe you could unpack them and clean them up. Could you find a place to display them which wouldn't bother your husband?

C: I guess I could use the spare office room. No one goes in there much.

T: When you started talking about the dolls you really lit up.

C: (laughs) Yeah, I know it's silly, but I forgot how much I loved to see those dolls. It was fun for me to collect them.

T: Have you thought about starting a business for buying and selling dolls?

Anna sits quietly for a period of time reflecting.

C: No, I haven't. I have never been business minded.

T: That is Ok. Maybe you are just one of those collectors who have a great deal of knowledge about something and other people turn to learn from?

C: I don't know. It has been years.

T: What would it be like for you to pull out those dolls again?

C: I would love it.

T: My gut tells me that you are missing that special quality that many of us miss. We enjoy things so much when we are young and then we think we have to grow up and put away things that brought us joy and gave us creativity. You know what I mean? It is like a part of us didn't need to stop enjoying things, but life came along and took it away.

C: Yeah.

T: I know many adult women who are very active working with dolls, collecting dolls and enjoying dolls as a hobby. It ties them to their childhood in a pleasant way. They still are very responsible grown-ups, but they are also able to have fun with things from the past. Nostalgia is not a bad thing.

C: I agree.

T: Porcelain dolls are interesting. They can be so fragile. It is like we need to treat them with care. Rather than boxing them up and forgetting about them, we may need to bring them out and honor their presence. Honoring them is kind of like honoring the old you. You can be very fragile, but yet you are still here and moving forward. Maybe these dolls need a special place that you alone get to enjoy them.

C: Right.

T: I wonder what your home will be like in the next two weeks when you are walking twenty minutes a day, have rearranged furniture, painted walls, put up family pictures, and have a special place for all your porcelain dolls?

C: It will be a big change.

T: Sure. Will it be a good change?

C: Yes, absolutely.

T: These changes will be a good way to channel that energy, won't it?

C: I think so. I really hadn't thought about those dolls in years. I had not realized how much I missed seeing them.

T: It is probably the same as your family have missed seeing you. This will be really cool that your family will get you back and you will get the dolls back.

C: Yeah.

Anna returned to therapy in three weeks. She stated she had completed all the tasks requested and did indeed feel more energetic than she had in a long time. She had given her dolls a special place in the spare office room. She also painted the one wall in the living room and put up family photographs on the wall. She remarked that her children were interested in the porcelain dolls, and she felt that their interest created a different bonding experience for them. She also started going to doll shops and taking short trips to find more porcelain dolls. Her husband was still uncomfortable around the dolls, but he was fine that the dolls were in a room he rarely ever went in. Anna admitted to occasionally feeling anxious and depressed, which she had taken as a sign for her to do something creative. Overall, she reported feeling more like herself and having a sense that she had "come home" to who she really is. Anna stated she was even considering setting up an online business to sell porcelain dolls.

REFERENCES

Armstrong, C. (2015). *The Therapeutic "Aha!": 10 Strategies for Getting Your Clients Unstuck.* New York: Norton.

Bateson, G. (1979). *Mind and Nature: A Necessary Unity.* London: Fontana.

Bateson, G. (1972). *Steps to an Ecology of Mind.* Chicago: University of Chicago Press.

Beutler, L. E., Malik, M., Alimohamed, S. Harwood. TM, Talebi, H., Noble, S. & Wong, E. (2004). Therapist variables. In Lambert, M.J. (ed.), *Bergin and Garfield's Handbook of Psychotherapy and Behavior Change* (pp. 227-306). New York: Wiley.

Blow, A.J., Sprenkle, D.H., & Davis, S.D. (2007). Is who delivers the treatment more important than the treatment itself? *Journal of Marital and Family Therapy, 33* (3), 298-317.

Boscolo, L. & Betrando, P. (1996). *Systemic Therapy with Individuals.* London: Karnac.

Corbett, L. (2001). *The Sacred Cauldron: Psychotherapy as a Spiritual Practice.* Wilmette, Ill:Chiron Publications.

Cozolino, L. (2004). *The Making of a Therapist: A Practical Guide for the Inner Journey.* New York: Norton.

Demartini, J. (2013). *The Values Factor: The Secret to Creating an Inspired and Fulfilling Life.* New York: Berkley.

Duncan, B.L., Miller, S.D., & Sparks, J. (2004). *The Heroic Client: A Revolutionary Way to Improve Effectiveness Through Client-directed, Outcome-informed Therapy.* San Francisco: Jossey-Bass.

Fife, S. T., Whiting, J. B., Bradford, K., & Davis, S. (2014). The therapeutic pyramid: A common factors synthesis of techniques, alliance, and way of being. *Journal of Marital and Family Therapy, 40 (*1), 20-33.

Fisch, R., Weakland, J.H., & Segal, L. (1982). *The Tactics of Change: Doing Therapy Briefly*. San Francisco: Jossey-Bass.

Frankl, V. (2006). *Man's Search for Meaning: An Introduction to Logotherapy*. Boston: Beacon Press.

Friedman, S. (1994). Staying simple, staying focused: Time-effective consultations with children and families. In Hoyt, M. (1994). *Constructive Therapies*. New York: Guilford 217 – 250.

Furman, B. & Ahola, T. (1994). Solution talk: The solution oriented way of talking about problems. In Hoyt, M. (1994). *Constructive Therapies*. New York: Guilford, 41-66.

Gillian, S. (1993). Therapeutic rituals: Passages into new identities. In Gilligan, S. & Price, R.(1993). *Therapeutic Conversations*. New York: Norton.

Gilligan, S.G. (1986). *Therapeutic Trances: The Co-Operation Principle in Ericksonian Hypnotherapy.* New York: Routledge,

Gordon, D. Meyers-Anderson, M. (1981). *Phoenix: Therapeutic Patterns of Milton H. Erickson*. Capitola, CA: Meta Publications.

Haley, J. & Richeport-Haley, M. (2003). *The Art of Strategic Therapy*. New York: Routledge.

Haley, J. (1990). *Strategies of Psychotherapy*. New York: Norton.

Haley, J. (1973). *Uncommon Therapy: The Psychiatric Techniques of Milton H. Erickson, M.D*. New York: Norton.

Keeney, B.P. (1983). *Aesthetics of Change*. Guilford: New York.

Keeney, B. (2009). *The Creative Therapist: The Art of Awakening a Session.* New York: Routledge.

Keeney, H. & Keeney, B. (2012). *Circular Therapeutics: Giving*

Therapy a Healing Heart. Phoenix: Zeig, Tucker & Theisen.

Lankton, S. (2001). Ericksonian Therapy. In Corsini, R. (Editor) *Handbook of Innovative Therapy*. 2nd Edition. 196-205. New York: Wiley

Lebrow, J. (2006). *Research for the Psychotherapist: From Science to Practice.* New York: Routledge.

Leslie, P.J. (2014). *Potential Not Pathology: Helping Your Clients Transform Using EricksonianPsychotherapy*. London: Karnac.

Madanes, C. (2006). *The Therapist as Humanist, Social Activist, and Systemic Thinker: and Other Selected Papers*. Phoenix: Zeig, Tucker, & Theisen.

Musikantow, R. (2011). Thinking in circles: Power and responsibility in hypnosis. *AmericanJournal of Clinical Hypnosis*, (54) 83-85.

Musikantow, R. (2015). A modeling of Bradford Keeney's ability to gain cooperation withdirectives. *The Qualitative Report,* 20 (11), 1737-1746.

Nardone, G. (1996). *Brief Strategic Solution-oriented Therapy of Phobic and Obsessive Disorders*. New Jersey: Jason Aronson, Inc.

O'Hanlon, B. (2014). *Out of the Blue: Six Non-medication Ways to Relieve Depression.* New York: Norton

O'Hanlon, B. (2003). *A Guide to Inclusive Therapy: 26 Methods of Respectful, Resistance-Dissolving Therapy.* New York: Norton.

Ray, W.A. & Kenney, B.P. (1993). *Resource-focused Therapy*. London: Karnac Books.

Rossi, E (2001). The Deep Psychobiology of Psychotherapy. In Corsini, R. (Editor) *Handbook of Innovative Therapy*. (2nd Ed.). 155-165. New York. Wiley

Sprenkle, D.H. & Blow, A.J. (2007). The role of the therapist as the bridge between common factors and therapeutic change: More complex than congruency with a worldview. *Journal of Family*

Therapy, 29, 109-113.

Watzlawick, P., Weakland, J.H., Fisch, R. (1974). *Change: Principles of Problem Formation and Problem Resolution.* New York: Norton.

Whitaker, C.A. & Bumberry, W.M. (1988). *Dancing with the Family: A Symbolic-experientialQW Approach.* New York: Routledge.

Yapko, M. (2001). *Treating Depression with Hypnosis.* New York: Routledge

www.ingramcontent.com/pod-product-compliance
Lightning Source LLC
Chambersburg PA
CBHW031519270326
41930CB00006B/430